MW00788636

HOW

to

STUDY

the

BIBLE

*A Straightforward Guide
to Understanding the Scriptures*

HOW
to
STUDY
the
BIBLE

A Straightforward Guide
to Understanding the Scriptures

BEN WILLIAMS

How to Study the Bible
A Straightforward Guide to Understanding the Scriptures
Copyright © 2023 by Ben Williams

Published by Lucid Books in Houston, TX
www.LucidBooks.com

SBN: 978-1-63296-649-0 (paperback)
ISBN: 978-1-63296-624-7 (hardback)
eISBN: 978-1-63296-625-4

Special Sales: Most Lucid Books titles are available in special quantity discounts. Custom imprinting or excerpting can also be done to fit special needs. Contact Lucid Books at Info@LucidBooks.com

For Aletheia

May you be a living testimony to the power of Bible study for your generation.
May the Word compel you to give your life for the glory of the Father.
May the Word cultivate within you a deep affection for the Son.
May the Word teach you what it means to walk in the Spirit.

Live up to your name, kiddo. Daddy loves you.

CONTENTS

INTRODUCTION

STUDY. PRACTICE. TEACH.

For Ezra had set his heart to study the law of the Lord *and to practice it, and to teach* His *statutes and ordinances in Israel.*

—Ezra 7:10

I'LL NEVER FORGET the first time I read Ezra 7:10. It was nearly eight years ago, and I was sitting in my dining room preparing a Sunday school lesson for the youth group at our church. I remember physically getting out of my chair and pacing back and forth a few times, trying to process what I had just read. *How had I never noticed this verse before?* The words hit me—hard. Walking back to my Bible, I read the verse again, this time more slowly. As I did, three words kept jumping out at me.

Study. Practice. Teach.

As I read the verse several more times, I realized that these were so much more than just black words on white paper. This was a blueprint, a road map to becoming the man God made me to be. The three words kept repeating in my head, and they summed up the life I was longing to lead.

Many of today's Christians are lost in a fog of confusion, wandering aimlessly through life without direction, clarity, or purpose. The consequences of that are staggering. Our society is more divided and combative than it's ever been. Many homes are broken. Many children are growing up without a model of Christ to pattern their lives after. Many Christians are languishing in the faith, missing out on the joy and victory that come with biblical maturity. And many churches are struggling to reach their communities that are already floundering without strong leadership.

The one glaring deficiency in our culture is the lack of Christ-followers who know the truth (study), live in obedience to the truth (practice), and passionately share the truth with others (teach). Every problem in society can trace its roots back to this void, and that's why I've written this book. I want to equip you to study the Bible for yourself because I'm confident that a return to the Bible will ignite a return to Jesus.

My humble prayer is that this book will stir something deep within you—a yearning to know God more through the Scriptures He's given you. I pray that you will fall more in love with Jesus than ever before and that you will know Him more deeply and intimately than ever. I pray that you persevere through the long and difficult days when you don't want to study the Bible or feel like spending time with God. I pray that you see the tangible fruit of Scripture changing your life. I pray that the pages of this book serve to launch you onto a path of spiritual growth that never ceases. How can all this happen? Because the Bible is no ordinary book. It's the living, active, and powerful Word of God, and it will turn your life upside down if you let it (Heb. 4:12).

Ben Williams
Macon, North Carolina
March 12, 2023

PART 1

HOW TO STUDY THE WORD

CHAPTER 1

OFTEN NEGLECTED, ALWAYS PROFITABLE

All Scripture is inspired by God and profitable for teaching, for reproof, for correction, for training in righteousness; so that the man of God may be adequate, equipped for every good work.
—2 Tim. 3:16–17

IF YOU REALLY engage with this book, it will change your life, not because of me—I'm nobody special—but because the topic we'll learn together is tremendously special. It has changed my life and the lives of countless others. It will change yours, too, if you're willing to devote yourself to what you'll learn in this book and give it some time.

Learning how to study the Bible is the single greatest lesson I've ever learned because it unlocked a multitude of other lessons that have radically changed my life. I've only been studying the Bible for about 12 years, and I'm simply amazed at how God has transformed my life since learning how to study the Bible for myself.

Through His Word, God has given me victory over addictions and sins that had previously ruled my life and kept me from walking in freedom. He's healed and transformed my marriage, which only a few years ago seemed broken beyond repair. He's given me the wisdom to navigate circumstances that would otherwise have led to my ruin. He's given me hope and called me to a purpose greater than I ever could have imagined. He's enabled me to forgive people I didn't think I could forgive. He's taught me the joy of humility and serving others. He's encouraged me when I felt discouraged and given me faith and hope when I saw no way forward. And in the process, I've come to know my Jesus intimately and truly. Through the Word, I have fallen more deeply in love with Jesus than ever before, and I sincerely can't wait for the day when I get to gaze into His eyes and see Him face to face (1 Cor. 13:12).

Please don't get me wrong—my Christian life still has more holes in it than Swiss cheese, but I'm hopeful because of all Christ has accomplished in me already. And I pray that the coming years yield even more growth, even more change, and even more fruit—for you and me both. Based on the verses at the beginning of this chapter, I'm confident that God will grant that request if we only devote ourselves wholeheartedly to studying, practicing, and teaching His Word. Let's look at what 2 Timothy 3:16–17 means.

The Word Is Inspired

The Bible contains every word that God wanted to say to us about who He is, who we are, and how much God loves us. In the Word, we see God's heart toward us in Christ, the way of salvation, and the ultimate victory of Jesus in eternity. How can any other book be more important than this?

Surely these truths make the Word more worthy of our time than the football games we mindlessly watch each weekend or the games we play for hours on our smartphones. If we're devoting significantly less time and attention to the Word than the things that feed our flesh, then aren't we missing something?

The Word Is Profitable

Scripture is the one investment that *always* yields a high return. Any time you invest in the Word is ultimately for your good. Every second you invest in Bible study is time that God can work to renew your mind and transform your heart into the likeness of Christ and equip you to better serve Him. From Genesis to Revelation, every word of the Word is worth studying. In a world that constantly bombards us and tempts us to waste our time with what is unprofitable, let us make our lives about what is most profitable—knowing Christ through His Word.

The Word Is Our Teacher

The Word is inspired and profitable for doctrine, or teaching. In other words, the Scriptures teach us what to believe and how to live out our faith in Christ. That is especially helpful for newer believers who are trying to wrap their minds around the fundamentals of the faith such as the death, burial, and resurrection of Jesus; the mission of the church; and the joys that await us in heaven.

But we all know that a person never "arrives" as a Christian. No matter how long you've walked with Christ, you're still in need of sitting at the feet of Jesus and learning from His Word. With the Holy Spirit as your teacher and guide, the Word shows us how to follow Jesus faithfully in this crazy, unpredictable world.

The Word Is Our Reprover

Scripture is also faithful to reprove us. In other words, it's faithful to call us out when we're walking away from God and going in the wrong direction. And this reproof is God's grace and love toward us, my friend. The Father longs for us to enjoy abundant life and intimate fellowship with Him, so He shows us where we are living in disobedience. If I'm struggling with pride, the Holy Spirit points me to scriptures that speak of the foolishness of pride and the importance of humility. If I'm struggling with lust, the Spirit directs me to scriptures that deal with the consequences of lust and the joy of pure and holy living.

In doing this, God isn't trying to shame me. He's trying to get my attention because He knows where pride or lust can take me if leave them unchecked in my life. He longs for me to know the abundant joy of walking in obedience, so He calls me away from these sins because He loves me too much to let them remain in me. He'll do the same for you as you dive into the Word.

The Word Is Our Corrector

A ruler not only shows what is crooked but also reveals what is straight. In the same way, God's Word not only exposes the crookedness of our hearts but also shows us how to replace that crookedness with right living so we can walk in the joy of obedience and intimacy with Christ.

For example, the Bible doesn't simply say, "You shall not steal" (Exod. 20:15). It also shows us how to turn from stealing and begin living in contentment as we trust in God as our provider. And Scripture doesn't merely command us to love our neighbors as ourselves (Matt. 22:39); it tangibly shows us how to live with genuine care and compassion for those around us. In doing that, the Word always gives us hope for a more abundant and obedient tomorrow, even if we've needed some reproof in the process.

The Word Is Our Instructor

The Word trains us in righteousness. This phrase in Greek literally refers to the process of raising children and training them up in the way they should go. Through His Word, God the Father trains and teaches us to walk in His ways and live in His will so our lives are pleasing to Him.

Are we so holy that we no longer need the training and instruction of the Word? Surely not. But if we're neglecting the Bible, we're neglecting being trained to fulfill our calling in Christ. After all, the Bible equips us to serve God well. It equips us to raise our own children faithfully. It equips us to make disciples and present them mature in Christ. It equips us to serve one another, forgive one another, and prefer one another in love. If we want to do those things well, we must receive consistent instruction from the Word.

The Word Is Our Equipper

In a sense, these four areas—teaching, reproof, correction, and instruction in righteousness—sum up the entire Christian life. At any given moment of your life with Christ, you're in need of one of those four things, which means that in every moment, the Word is profitable and has something to teach you so you might be "adequate, equipped for every good work" (2 Tim. 3.17).

The Greek word translated *adequate* carries the idea of being perfectly suited for the job. If you've ever worked in a job in construction or home repair, you know how important it is to have the right tools for the job. If you need to take a measurement, your tape measure is the right tool for the job. If you need to pound some nails, a hammer is perfectly suited for the task. In the same way, Paul tells us that the Bible's design is to make us adequate, or perfectly suited for the good works that God has prepared in advance for us to do (Eph. 2:10). The Scriptures may not make you perfect at everything, but they'll perfectly prepare you for the life God has called you to.

Why We Must Study the Word

At this point, you may be thinking, "Can't I grow by simply reading the Bible?" And the answer is *absolutely*! In no way do I want to downplay the importance of reading Scripture. There are many excellent Bible reading plans and programs that are designed to help you become more acquainted with the Bible as a whole, and I would heartily recommend that you use them. However, Bible study serves a different purpose in our spiritual growth. Reading Scripture exposes us to large quantities of the Bible; studying Scripture takes us deeper into the truth of God's Word.

Typically, I recommend Bible *reading* for those who are newer to the faith and want to take in large quantities of the Bible over the course of a year or several years. But at some point, as the Christian matures, there should be a desire for greater depth of understanding, and that is when I highly encourage Bible *study* as a means of additional growth in the faith. It is when we learn to study the Bible that our roots really begin to deepen, and our relationship with God grows to a whole new level. Let's consider how that works in the next chapter.

CHAPTER 2

A TWO-PERSON ACTIVITY

But the Helper, the Holy Spirit, whom the Father will send in My name, He will teach you all things, and bring to your remembrance all that I said to you.

—John 14:26

PERHAPS THE BIGGEST reason we miss the mark with Bible study is that we fail to understand what is really happening when we study the Word. For a long time, I endeavored to study the Bible on my own as a sort of duty to God. I figured that if I worked hard to study the Word, I would learn more about God and the Christian life. As a result, God would be pleased with me and help me live out whatever new things I'd learned, and that's how I would grow spiritually.

For years, my approach to the Bible was one giant act of the flesh. I can't tell you how many times I studied the Bible only to walk away frustrated and discouraged. I couldn't figure out how to understand the Bible or how to live it. It felt hopeless. Later, I discovered that with the approach I was taking, it really was hopeless.

By attempting to study the Bible apart from the Holy Spirit, I was dooming myself to a fully human interaction with the divine Word of God. It was just me, the Bible, and the arrogant assumption that I could understand and live out the truths of the Bible on my own. But as I began to study with the Spirit as my Guide, placing myself under Him as my Teacher, everything began to change. The truth became clearer and more powerful in my life. It was as if the Spirit was teaching me things I couldn't have understood on my own and then making those truths a very part of me. The Spirit began opening my eyes, giving me understanding, and making the truths of Scripture a life-changing reality in my mind and heart.

I pray that God opens your eyes to see that Bible study is so much more than looking up keywords or discovering historical and cultural context. It's a supernatural interaction with the Spirit of God who authored the Word and dwells within us. Let's examine how that works, and may God give us a higher view of our need for the Spirit when we study the Bible.

We Never Study the Bible Alone

Don't miss this, my friend. Every time you sit down to study your Bible, you're engaging in a two-person activity. It's designed to be a back-and-forth interaction between you and the Spirit of God. If only I'd known that during my first few years of learning to study the Bible! The Word never returns void, but so much of what I studied fell on deaf ears due to my own ignorance. I was trying to study the Word *for* God instead of *with* God.

Don't get me wrong. I was going through every step I'm about to share with you in the next chapter. I checked all the boxes, but I was checking them without God, and that is why the truth never quite sunk in. How many of our Bible studies fail to yield fruit because we miss this?

Bible study done in communion with the Spirit of Almighty God will not leave us the same. So, as we study, let's assume our places as humble, meek, and lowly students, acknowledging that we cannot understand even the simplest truths of Scripture unless God's Spirit makes them clear to us. The Spirit then acts as our teacher and guide. As we submit to the Spirit in faith, He does the work in us. Let's examine all He will do for us as we study if only we allow Him to have His rightful place in our hearts.

The Spirit Inspired the Word

Don't miss God's grace in this. Who is better to act as our teacher and guide as we study Scripture than the One who authored it in the first place? The Spirit of Christ who dwells in the believer moment by moment, day by day, is the same Spirit who inspired the authors of Scripture as they wrote. And He dwells in us to make the Word clear to us, to work in us the character of Jesus, and to empower us for a life of obedience.

The Spirit came upon the minds of Moses, David, Paul, Matthew, Peter, Luke, Ezra, and so many others as they penned the words that are now before us in the Scriptures. Each one, writing with their own style and personality, was fully under the inspiration of God's Spirit as they wrote. And if they needed the Spirit to write the Word, why do we assume that we can understand it without the Spirit?

The Spirit Teaches Us the Word

When we study in our own power without the Spirit as our teacher and guide, we're leaning on our own understanding and trusting in ourselves to comprehend and live out the Word. But the flesh can't impart truth to itself any more than death can impart life to itself.

God, help us realize that if we are to understand the Bible, then understanding cannot come from within—it must be imparted to us. Only the Holy Spirit can unfold the majesty of the gospel to the cold heart that needs salvation. Only the Holy Spirit can reveal to each Christian "what is the hope of His calling, what are the riches of the glory of His inheritance in the saints, and what is the surpassing greatness of His power toward us who believe" (Eph. 1:18–19).

If you long to know God more through His Word, remove all trust in yourself. None of us would attempt to climb Mount Everest without a guide, and neither should we attempt to study the Scriptures without the Spirit who will guide us into "all the truth" (John 16:13). You cannot imagine all the Spirit has for you if you will only humbly submit yourself to the Holy Spirit as your teacher. We'll unpack these realities more in the chapters ahead.

The Spirit Convicts Us through the Word

> *But I tell you the truth, it is to your advantage that I go away;*
> *for if I do not go away, the Helper will not come to you; but if I*
> *go, I will send Him to you. And He, when He comes, will convict*
> *the world concerning sin and righteousness and judgment.*
> —John 16:7–8

To study the Word without the Spirit is to study the Word without being convicted of sin, *and that is simply terrifying.* When we study in our own wisdom, the Scriptures are still faithful to show us our sin, but the end result within us amounts to either indifference toward our sin ("it's not that big of a deal") or despair because of our sin ("I'll never live a life of victory"). Only with the Spirit as our guide will we see our sin for what it is (Ps. 139:23–24), mourn over it (Matt. 5:4), and seek His aid in faith as we put to death the deeds of the flesh (Rom. 8:13).

The Spirit Transforms Us through the Word

Bible study is far, far more than an academic exercise. God's goal is always to transform the believer, working in us the nature and character of Jesus Christ. For God, the goal of Bible study isn't simply to give us new knowledge or understanding. God's purpose is to reveal more of Himself to us each time we study, resulting in life transformation that comes from a changed heart and brings glory to His name. If that is His goal, then shouldn't it also be ours?

Only the Spirit who lives in us and teaches us the Word can work to bring about this lasting change in us. Our place is to yield to His working in us and allow Him to transform us from the inside out as we study. Only then will we consistently live in victory, walk in love, and bear fruit that is pleasing to God.

The Spirit Empowers Us to Obey the Word

Our flesh will fail us. If Bible study attempted in self-effort falls short, then won't the obedience attempted in self-effort fall short as well? And yet this is exactly how many of us attempt to live for God. Do we really believe that human willpower can create and sustain a life of obedience?

How many Christians put in a tremendous, sincere effort to study and obey the Word only to wallow in spiritual failure and defeat? Many of us have wonderful intentions and are genuinely trying to obey God, but we have yet to learn that even our best efforts to live for God are powerless if we haven't first let God's Spirit transform our hearts and empower our living. Allow Andrew Murray's words to drive this point home in your heart.

> A man cannot live one hour a godly life unless by the power of the Holy Spirit. He may live a proper, consistent life, as people call it, an irreproachable life, a life of virtue and diligent service; but to live a life acceptable to God, in the enjoyment of God's salvation and God's love, to live and walk in the power of the new life—he cannot do it unless he be guided by the Holy Spirit every day and every hour.[1]

Only the Spirit can set us free from the law of sin and death (Rom. 8:2). Only the Spirit enables us to put to death the deeds of the flesh (Rom. 8:13). Only the Spirit can produce in us the lasting fruit of love, joy, peace, patience, kindness, goodness, faithfulness, gentleness, and self-control (Gal. 5:22–23). We will live in His power only as we yield ourselves to Him.

The Spirit Reminds Us of the Word

I firmly believe that one of the Spirit's greatest ministries is to remind us of the Word. Can you imagine how difficult it would be to navigate life well without the consistent, gentle reminders that we receive from the Spirit?

How many times has He brought to our memory the exact truths we needed, precisely when we needed them? How many times has He delivered us from making poor, unwise choices through His promptings that remind us of the truth? Praise God for His divine nudges that direct us in the path of obedience.

The Spirit Helps Us Communicate the Word

We miss out on countless blessings when we study the Bible considering only how it might affect our lives. God reveals His Word to us for the good of others as much as for our own good. He intentionally places us in situations that provide us with opportunities to share what we're learning with others. And the Spirit who orchestrates these divine appointments is willing and ready to give us the words to say as we share what He has taught us.

The Spirit-Filled Life

The Spirit guides our study and teaches us the Word. He convicts us of sin, transforms our hearts, and empowers our obedience to God. He reminds us of the Word and helps us pass on the truth to others. The Spirit is crucial in every area of our Bible study. But more than that, He is crucial in every area of our lives.

Bible study is a two-person activity because the entire Christian life is a two-person activity. We study the Bible in tune with the Spirit because we are to do all things in tune with the Spirit. At no point are we meant to attempt Bible study or any area of the Christian life alone. To do so would be to quench the Spirit, and many of us are unknowingly guilty of this sin.

The way we interact with the Holy Spirit in Bible study is often a reflection of the way we interact with the Spirit in our daily lives. The Christian who devotes themselves to Spirit-filled living will naturally enjoy the sweet fruits of Spirit-led Bible study. However, the Christian who foolishly believes they can study and understand the Word apart from the Spirit's teaching will also believe they can deny self and follow Christ apart from the Spirit's sanctifying power.

Every moment of every day—whether I'm studying the Bible, at work, or at home with my family—Christ's Spirit is to be my guide, and my place is to humbly follow His lead. As I constantly receive from Him all I need to honor God, He empowers me to love my neighbors, make disciples, and conduct myself in a way that pleases the Father (John 7:37–39). That is what it means to enjoy the abundant life of intimate fellowship with Jesus our King.

My friend, listen to me. The Spirit-filled life is not out of reach, and neither is Spirit-led Bible study. But we cannot attempt either one alone. If you're a follower of Jesus, your entire life is a two-person activity. Now that we have this framework to guide us, let's learn how to study the Bible.

CHAPTER 3

EIGHT STEPS TO UNDERSTANDING THE SCRIPTURES

So will My word be which goes forth from My mouth;
it will not return to Me empty,
Without accomplishing what I desire,
And without succeeding in the matter *for which I sent it.*

—Isa. 55:11

NOW THAT WE'VE seen the importance of Bible study and the Holy Spirit's role as our teacher and guide, we're ready to examine the process we'll be using to study the Bible. The steps I'm about to lay out for you are not a magic formula. As we've already seen, you can do these things in the right order and still miss the boat in Bible study.

Many of us want to become more proficient in studying the Bible but don't know where to begin. Let me encourage you to use this as a template to get you started. As you become more familiar with each step, you may want to tweak this process and do a few things differently—and that's okay. This is how *I* study the Bible, but by no means is this the *only* way to study the Bible. I've spent years refining this process for myself, and it may be helpful for you to prayerfully consider how you might do the same. In this chapter, I'll provide an overview of the template we'll be using to study the Word together, and in the chapters ahead we'll unpack each step of the process more fully.

Prepare for the Word – Am I Ready to Hear from God?

This is perhaps the most important component of Bible study and also the most overlooked part. We all have a dangerous tendency to rush into our time with God, treating our time in His sacred Word as nothing more than another task to check off our list. We hinder our Bible study before it even begins because we hurry into the Word without pausing to remind ourselves of the tremendous weight of what's happening as we study.

Should we really approach Bible study with such a lack of thought and reverence? God deserves more of us. Before even cracking open our Bibles, we need to pause and prepare our hearts to hear from God.

Analyze the Word – What Does It Say?

It is also common to hinder our Bible study by skimming quickly over the verses in front of us so we can "get in another chapter." But how much truth did we really take in?

Like a detective at a crime scene, our first task in Bible study is to collect evidence and clues about what is being said. What words are being used? Are any of them repeated? What information can we gather about the author, the recipients, or even the time frame the verses of the Bible were written in?

The more information we gather during the analyzing stage, the easier our interpretation and application will be later on. My encouragement is to analyze every passage for twice as long as you think you need to.

Interpret the Word – What Does It Mean?

Once we've analyzed the Word and collected information about our passage, our natural response will be to ask questions. Why did the author say this? What are they trying to communicate? What does that word or phrase really mean? How did the original hearers interpret this? Answering these questions will help us understand what our passage means.

Interpreting the Word is the most dangerous of the steps in studying the Bible. So when we arrive at that step, we'll proceed with caution. If we haven't prepared our hearts or analyzed well, then we could easily come to incorrect conclusions about our passage and fall into error.

Meditate on the Word – Why Does This Matter?

It's not uncommon to faithfully prepare our hearts, analyze, and interpret the Word and still have major questions that remain unanswered or important parts of the passage that are still unclear to us. At that point, many Christians throw in the towel and move on to an easier part of the Bible. But some of the most precious truths in Scripture are reserved for those who meditate on the Word.

Meditating on the Word isn't mystical. It simply refers to taking time to ponder, consider, and pray through the passage, asking, "God, what am I still missing? Why is this still not clear to me? And why does this passage matter so much for our lives that You included it in Your Word?" The answers to these questions are often reserved for those who wait on the Lord to reveal them as they faithfully abide in the Word.

Apply the Word – What Should I Do?

As we study, we'll humbly ask God to show us how we need to change and how we should live differently as a result of what we're learning. Once we uncover the meaning of a passage, we'll naturally begin to take stock of our hearts and compare ourselves to what we're seeing in the Word.

Thankfully, some passages will remind us to keep doing something we're already doing well. Studying these sections of Scripture leaves us feeling encouraged and deeply thankful for God's grace in our lives. However, other passages may ask us to make major changes in our lives. In those moments, applying the Word will serve as the test of whether or not we really believe what we've just learned and whether we're willing to follow our Lord and Savior regardless of what He asks us to do.

Memorize the Word – When Will I Need This?

Most of us don't have our Bibles at our sides throughout the day, so it's important to commit to memory what we're learning in the Word. That allows the Spirit to help us remember it later on when we're faced with a difficult decision or have an opportunity to share what we've learned with someone else.

For some of us, Scripture memory comes rather easily, and for others it's a difficult task. Regardless of how easily you can retain information, we'll take a look at some practical tips to help you memorize Scripture more quickly and effectively.

Pray the Word – What Can Only God Do?

Every time we study a passage, we should walk away with at least one prayer request. In almost every passage of Scripture, there is a beautiful balance between what God is to do in me and for me, and what I am to do for Him. Many of our failures in the Christian life stem from not knowing the difference between the two. When this happens, we try to do God-things for God instead of letting Him accomplish His work in us.

On the other hand, there are often elements of Scripture that we are responsible to live out. There are commands to obey, truths to uphold, and principles to live by. In these cases, it is helpful to pray for God's grace and favor as we labor and strive to live in obedience through the Spirit's power.

Teach the Word – Who Can I Share This With?

When most of us think of teaching the Bible, we picture a Sunday school teacher, a seminary professor, or a pastor behind a pulpit. But in reality, most Bible teaching happens in normal, everyday conversations where followers of Jesus share how Scripture has set them free and given them life. Every day we interact with dozens of people who desperately need to hear what God has taught us by His grace, and God's design is for all of us to be Bible teachers in those daily conversations.

The Mindset of Patient Perseverance

Let me be clear before we begin unpacking this process in greater depth. You can't skim through these steps quickly and hope to study the Word well. Bible study requires time and a patient, thorough approach. It shouldn't be approached with a task-oriented mindset but rather a growth-oriented mindset.

A task-oriented mindset is focused on getting through these steps quickly instead of thoroughly. Its primary goal is to check off the "quiet time" box so we can get on with our day, and it is content with whatever growth happens in the process.

A growth-oriented mindset isn't afraid to study the same passage for a few days or even weeks, if necessary. Instead of giving up and moving on when Bible study becomes difficult or takes longer than we'd like, a growth-oriented mindset is willing to do whatever it takes to understand what God is saying to us in His Word. It chooses to persevere until God makes clear what we need to know in order to please Him. It refuses to forfeit the precious truths God reserves for those who are willing to abide in the Word.

Our Passage – James 1:21–25

In the pages ahead, we will examine each of these eight steps in greater detail and begin putting them into practice as we study James 1:21–25. Before we move on, let's take a look at the passage we'll be studying together.

Therefore, putting aside all filthiness and all that remains of wickedness, in humility receive the word implanted, which is able to save your souls. But prove yourselves doers of the word, and not merely hearers who delude themselves. For if anyone is a hearer of the word and not a doer, he is like a man who looks at his natural face in a mirror; for once he has looked at himself and gone away, he has immediately forgotten what kind of person he was. But one who looks intently at the perfect law, the law of liberty, and abides by it, not having become a forgetful hearer but an effectual doer, this man will be blessed in what he does.

—James 1:21–25

Take your time throughout the rest of this book. Commit to the entire process. Each Bible study step builds on the previous one, so there are no short-cuts on this journey to spiritual growth. Because Bible study begins in the heart and not the head, we'll begin by preparing our hearts to hear from God.

CHAPTER 4

PREPARE FOR THE WORD

For the word of God is living and active and sharper than any two-edged sword, and piercing as far as the division of soul and spirit, of both joints and marrow, and able to judge the thoughts and intentions of the heart.

—Heb. 4:12

NOW THAT WE know which passage of Scripture we'll be studying—James 1:21–25—our natural inclination is to dive immediately into each verse, picking apart every word and trying to understand what it means (and perhaps you've already started). However, before we endeavor to understand our passage, we must first ensure that we're coming to the Word with the right mindset. After all, the attitude with which we approach the Word is significant and often determines the outcome of our Bible study before it even begins. And unfortunately, this first step of Bible study quite often becomes our downfall.

The one major reason we struggle with Bible study is that we fail to connect rightly with God who longs to speak to us through His Word as we study. Remember, above all, Bible study is *relational*. Only when we make knowing God and connecting with God our greatest aim will we grasp the truth and allow God to impress it upon our hearts.

Many of us take a nonchalant, carefree approach to Bible study that demonstrates a distracted heart. I know I have done that more times than I would like to admit. It saddens me to think of how many times I've been glued to a post on social media or read a news article with rapt attention, only to turn around and approach Bible study as if it were no more interesting or important than math homework.

Countless others are distracted in a different way. I am particularly burdened for the seminary students, pastors, theologians, and Bible scholars who study with a purely academic mindset as if the inspired Word of God is nothing more than a textbook that contains truths for us to work into our lectures and sermons. While we must study the Word faithfully and accurately, how often have we pored over the Scriptures in such a way that enlarges the head and yet starves the heart? Are we allowing our search for answers to distract us from seeking God Himself?

Surely, we who lead in the church have much to repent of in this area. Have we not often valued the truths of Scripture more highly than the God who authored them? May God open our eyes to see how often we have learned concepts from the Bible without really coming "to the knowledge of the truth" (2 Tim. 3:7).

Think about all of this from God's perspective. Would you and I want to share our most intimate thoughts with someone who is distracted? Would we bare our souls to someone who is only interested in our answers to their selfish questions? Absolutely not! And we shouldn't expect that God will either.

Don't miss the implications of this. We do not learn the Bible to the degree that we follow the eight steps outlined in the previous chapter. We do not understand the Bible to the degree that we are smart or diligent or have good intentions. We will lay hold of the Scriptures to the degree that we are intent on laying hold of God. He is our prize, not answers, in Bible study.

Our Bible study will only yield fruit to the degree that we are in tune with the Spirit of Christ as we study. Those who seek Him with all their heart will find Him in His Word, but those who seek only to understand His Word will doom themselves to missing both God and the truth. So let us set our attention and affections on God as we study. He longs to reveal Himself to us through His Word because He delights in intimate fellowship with His children. Before we dive into James 1:21–25, here are a few ways to prepare yourself to meet with Christ as you study under the direction of His Spirit.

TIPS FOR THE DISTRACTED MIND

Remove Anything That Hinders Your Focus

Pastor and author A. W. Tozer once said, "Whatever keeps me from my Bible is my enemy, however harmless it may appear to be."[2] That's so true. When we study with a distracted mind, we are incapable of grasping all that God has to teach us. Intimate fellowship with the Almighty happens in secret as we remove ourselves from the busyness of daily life to meet alone with the Father. Nothing should compete with God for our attention and affection, so put down the phone, turn off the TV, and get away from the noise.

This is why I prefer to study the Bible in the morning before work. There are fewer interruptions when I get up before the rest of the household begins to stir, and it's far easier for me to stay focused on God. If I'm in bed by 10:00 p.m. (and let's be honest, few edifying things happen after 10:00 p.m. anymore), I can easily be awake by 6:00 a.m., which gives me plenty of quiet, uninterrupted time with my Jesus.

Regardless of when you spend time with Christ in His Word, guard yourself ruthlessly against distractions. No email is more important than what your Father wants to show you. No upcoming appointment is as precious as the one you're keeping with your Savior and King. And no problems you'll face today are worth worrying about when you can give them to Almighty God in prayer. Be vigilant—our minds cannot be filled with the Word when they're already half full of the cares or entertainment of this world.

Repent of Unconfessed Sin

Nothing hinders our Bible study more than unconfessed sin, and yet how often we have attempted to study the Word in this state. Many of us are floundering in our Bible studies, unable to receive new life from the Word because we have refused to respond in humility to the Spirit's conviction.

Do we really believe that we can live in open and unconfessed disobedience and yet feast on the pure truths of Scripture? Do we actually think we can enjoy fellowship with God in His Word while continually breaking fellowship with Him in our daily living? If so, we lie to ourselves.

But see God's grace in this. He will not allow us to enjoy intimate fellowship with Him through His Word until we have dealt with our sins. With repentance and humility come renewed intimacy and sweet fellowship with Almighty God in His Word.

My friend, the sin that hinders your relationship with God will hinder your Bible study, but wherever the Spirit convicts you, God's forgiveness and mercy are available in full. If you've been living in sin, bow yourself before the Father in humility and brokenness, confess your sins to Him in full, and receive the comfort of forgiveness and restoration.

Give Thanks in Worship

I'm *that* guy. I play the same few worship songs on repeat for months on end, making my family and closest friends want to pull their ears off or dive out of my moving vehicle just to get away. In fact, if you and I hung out for a few hours and I turned on Spotify, I can almost guarantee that you'll hear each of the songs below.

"Always Good" – Andrew Peterson
"I Shall Not Want" – Audrey Assad
"Crown Him" – I Am They
"Christ Has Risen" (Acoustic Sessions) – Phil Wickham
"Heaven Song" – Phil Wickham
"Here with Me" (Acoustic) – Phil Wickham
"I CHOOSE TO WORSHIP" – Rend Collective
"Psalm 8" – Shane & Shane
"My Portion" – Shane & Shane

Worshiping God through music is not only helpful to give us the right perspective throughout our day, but it has a way of setting the tone for our time in Bible study as well. Worship reminds us of the majesty of our Savior and prepares our hearts to receive all He has to teach us.

Commit to Obedience in Advance

Please don't skim past this. If I could point to one thing that has radically transformed my Bible study, it would be to commit to obedience in advance. Typically, we like to study the Bible, learn what it means, and then decide whether or not we'll obey its teaching, as if disobedience were an option for us as followers of Jesus. Rather than submit to the authority of the Word, we often argue with it, rationalizing and justifying why our lives are the exception and why we do not need to conform to the truth. Then we wonder why our Bible study is fruitless. It's because we're quenching the Spirit who desires us to walk in obedience.

Before I open the Word each day, I spend time in concentrated prayer, renewing my surrender and refusing to continue until I can honestly say I'll follow God's Word, regardless of what it says. Spending this time yielding to the Father in prayer has completely changed my time with Him in His Word. Don't get me wrong. It's often difficult to make the changes God asks of me in the moment, but in the end, I'm striving to live my life God's way because it is no longer I who live but Christ who lives in me (Gal. 2:20).

Because of this, our studies in the Word have led my wife and me to make decisions that at first seemed scary or uncomfortable. We've moved into a rougher section of our town so we can interact with people you wouldn't typically see in church. We've invited people to live in our home for free so we can both provide and enjoy a genuine Christian community for people our age. And we started a house church and nonprofit organization because we sense God calling us to equip Christ-followers to study, practice, and teach the Word.

I'm not sharing this to sound hyper-spiritual. If you could see everything in my heart for just one day, you'd be terribly disappointed in me. But I serve a great God who knows what is best for His children, and while obedience is often scary, I can honestly say I've never regretted committing to obedience in advance. God's way has often been hard, but it has always been best.

So, before you study, take time to submit yourself wholly to God. Commit to obeying whatever you will learn from Him through the Word. Before even knowing how God will teach and convict you, give Him your surrender, your allegiance, and your obedience up front. Then see if He won't reveal more of His heart to you through His Word.

Determine Not to Quit

Determining not to quit is easier said than done, right? You and I tend to give up as soon as discipline becomes difficult, especially when it comes to spiritual disciplines. How many prayer journals have we started only to give up after a few weeks or months? How many Bible reading plans have we abandoned once we ran into Leviticus or Numbers? And how many times have we started studying a book of the Bible only to leave it unfinished when we hit a roadblock in our studies?

My friend, discipline is always difficult, and Bible study is no exception. Dense and difficult passages can take weeks to study. Some books of the Bible can take years to work through. Late nights wrapped up in early mornings can leave us feeling physically exhausted and lacking in motivation. Life's trials and temptations can leave us spiritually drained and without any desire for God or His Word.

Yet it is in these seasons that the strength of our spiritual lives is truly forged. When we feel weakest, God's Word reminds us to trust in His strength and power—a truth that can carry us through the darkest seasons of our lives (2 Cor. 12:7–10). When we feel overwhelmed, Scripture reminds us that in Christ we can find rest for our weary souls. That gives us hope and confidence for each new day (Matt. 11:28–30). When our Father feels distant, His Word reminds us that He is near and that His nearness is our good (Ps. 73:28). And when we can't see a way forward in life, the Word reminds us to hope in God, for we will yet praise Him for His goodness (Ps. 42, 43).

Preparation Sets the Tone

Before we begin our study of James 1:21–25, let me encourage you to put this step into practice right now. Set down the book and turn off or put away anything that might compete for your attention. Set your heart completely on God. Come to Him in reverence and faith. Humble yourself before Him and ask Him to reveal more of Himself to you as you study our passage. Make knowing and loving Him your greatest aim for this study. Confess your sins to Him and turn from them. Commit to obedience in advance and determine that you will complete this undertaking in its entirety. Take as much time as you need, and when you're ready, I'll see you in the next chapter.

CHAPTER 5

ANALYZE THE WORD;
KNOW WHAT TO LOOK FOR

Open my eyes, that I may behold
Wonderful things from Your law.

—Ps. 119:18

WHEN YOU'RE FIRST learning how to study the Bible, it feels like you're staring at a *Where's Waldo?* picture with no Waldo. You know there's something important for you to see, but you're not sure where to look or how to find it. You're *looking* at the words, but you're struggling to *see* the biblical realities that are staring right back at you. You're taking time to read the Bible, but you're struggling to comprehend what God is trying to say. The truths of Scripture are so close, and yet you feel so far from being able to comprehend them. But take heart, my friend. Bible study is not a lost cause, and it doesn't need to be frustrating.

Consider for a moment what it is that typically makes Bible study frustrating for you. When I'm teaching groups how to study the Bible, I typically hear one of these two answers:

1. I don't know where to start, and I get overwhelmed, so I practically quit before I even get started.
2. I do start to study, but I get stuck because I don't know which parts of a passage are most important. Even if I did know what was most important, I wouldn't know what to do from there.

In other words, our greatest need is knowing what to look for. For example, where should we start with James 1:21–25? What should we focus on? Which details or words are most important? And how can we know whether we're understanding the passage or going off into heresy? Typically, these questions answer themselves as we take time to analyze the Word.

Analyzing the Word

Now that we've prepared our hearts to hear from God, we want to familiarize ourselves with our passage as much as possible. At least—and I'm not exaggerating—85 percent of effective Bible study comes down to *observation*, the ability to see the important details of a passage.

So, picture yourself as an investigator looking for clues at a crime scene. *Anything* could be important, and we have to assume that *everything* in our passage is important. You must be vigilant to find all the pieces of the puzzle. After all, the more puzzle pieces you're missing, the more difficult it will be to put the picture together in the end.

Generally speaking, the more time you spend analyzing your passage, the more accurate (and easy) your interpretation, application, and teaching will be. One of the primary dangers I see new students of the Bible making is that they want to look at the verse for about three minutes and then start interpreting and applying it right away. But remember, the key is to devote most of your time to the first four steps of the process. Let me encourage you to analyze the passage for twice as long as you think you need to.

At first, this will make Bible study feel painfully slow. But that's okay. Perhaps we've become used to studying the Bible too quickly. One of the most important things I've learned about Bible study is that the truth is rarely seen by those who are hasty and hurried. Understanding our passage requires that we have a patient, thorough approach.

Simple Exercises to Sharpen Your Mind

One of the simple practices that has helped me most with Bible study is doing Spot the Differences puzzles or other visual challenges that test my ability to observe, analyze, and think outside the box. I love tackling these challenges because they force me to look at the whole picture while also analyzing each of the components. That often requires me to look slowly and carefully at each picture from multiple angles in order to consider various points of view (something you'll find to be of immense value in Bible study).

For the rest of this chapter, take some time to work through the visual challenges below, and train yourself to do more than just *look*. Observe everything you can until you've *seen* the important details. Once you've completed the challenges, we'll learn how to apply these skills to Bible study. And if you get stuck, don't worry. The answer key is in Appendix A. Have fun!

Spot the Differences

There are five differences between the two pictures.

Can you find them?

How Many Squares Do You See?

Your Answer: _____

Can You Find Both of the Women in This Picture?

Spot the Differences

Let's make it a bit harder this time.
Can you find 8 differences between these two pictures?

Spot Eight Differences

One final test. Can you find 8 differences below?

Analyzing the Bible

Now that we've honed our observation skills, let's consider how that might be helpful when studying the Bible. There are two areas of Bible study where analyzing the Word is key. Let's consider them briefly before doing a deeper dive in the following chapters.

Analyze the Context

We cannot understand a passage without first understanding the context in which it was written. After all, the words of the Bible were written by and for people who lived in a different time in history, in a different location geographically, and in a different cultural setting than ours. Thus, we will err if we approach the Bible as 21st-century Westerners. If we don't immerse ourselves in their world, we may miss the meaning of a passage. In fact, there are many sections of Scripture that simply cannot be understood without knowledge of the historical or biblical context they were written in. We will learn more about analyzing the context of a passage in the next three chapters.

Analyze the Wording

Of all the possible modes and methods of communication God could have chosen, He specifically chose to reveal Himself to us through *words*. Thus, it is vital that we understand the words God uses to describe Himself, tell about us, and share the grand story of redemption that we find ourselves immersed in. Words have meaning, and the words of the supernatural God of the universe have supernatural meaning. We are wise to study them faithfully, and may the Spirit guide us into all truth as we do (John 16:13). We will learn more about doing word studies in Chapters 9–11.

Now It's Your Turn

Before we get into the next chapter, take some time to examine our passage more closely, and write down 20 of your own observations. Remember, we aren't coming to conclusions about what our passage means yet; we're simply observing and gathering information that will help us interpret it well later in the process.

As you analyze, feel free to highlight, underline, and circle any words that might seem important to you. Make notes in the margins as thoughts come to you and get as familiar with the passage as you can. I know that 20 observations

ANALYZE THE WORD; KNOW WHAT TO LOOK FOR

might seem like a lot, but the more you see now, the easier the rest of our Bible study will be. Once you have 20 observations (I took the liberty of writing the first two for you), I'll see you in the next chapter where we'll begin unpacking the context.

> *Therefore, putting aside all filthiness and all that remains of wickedness, in humility receive the word implanted, which is able to save your souls. But prove yourselves doers of the word, and not merely hearers who delude themselves. For if anyone is a hearer of the word and not a doer, he is like a man who looks at his natural face in a mirror; for once he has looked at himself and gone away, he has immediately forgotten what kind of person he was. But one who looks intently at the perfect law, the law of liberty, and abides by it, not having become a forgetful hearer but an effectual doer, this man will be blessed in what he does.*
>
> —James 1:21–25

Your Observations of James 1:21–25

1. The hearers of the Word delude themselves (verse 22).

2. Doers of the Word are blessed in what they do (verse 25).

3. _____

4. _____

5. _____

6. _____

7. _____

8. _____

9. _____

10. _____

11. _____

12. _____

13. _____

37

14. _____

15. _____

16. _____

17. _____

18. _____

19. _____

20. _____

CHAPTER 6

HISTORICAL CONTEXT – PART 1

The unfolding of Your words gives light;
It gives understanding to the simple.

—Ps. 119:130

AFTER OUR HEARTS are prepared to meet with God through His Word, we want to begin by seeking to understand the context of our passage. You see, we often miss key insights from the Word because we fail to consider the setting in which it was written. After all, the words of the Bible were not written in a vacuum. The Word was inspired by God and written by real people who lived in a real time of history. Studying the Bible without considering both the passage and its context is like eating pie without ice cream, a questionable choice indeed.

Pastor and author Pete Briscoe illustrates this point quite powerfully. Read the paragraph below and see if you can make sense of it without knowing the context.

> A newspaper is better than a magazine. A sea shore is a better place than the street. At first, it's better to run than to walk. You may have to try several times. It takes some skill, but it's easy to learn. Once successful, complications are minimal. Even young children can enjoy it. Birds seldom get too close. Rain, however, soaks in very fast. Too many people doing the same thing can cause problems. One needs a lot of room. If there are no complications, it can be very peaceful. A rock will serve as an anchor. If things break loose from it, however, you will not get a second chance.[3]

Were you able to figure it out without the context? I love riddles, so when I first heard this one, my mind kicked into hyperdrive trying to figure out what it was talking about. Sadly, after several minutes, all I had to show for myself was a headache. I just couldn't get it—until he shared the *context* of the paragraph. Then everything made perfect sense. Go back and read it again one more time, but this time read it while thinking of a *kite*.

It's remarkable how helpful context can be. Knowing the context of our passage in James 1 will prove to be even more powerful. If we don't take time to learn the context as we study the Bible, it's likely that we will walk away with little more than a headache. However, if we can devote ourselves to learning and understanding the context, our passage will become much easier to understand.

For example, consider these well-known verses from Revelation 3.

> *I know your deeds, that you are neither cold nor hot; I wish that you were cold or hot. So because you are lukewarm and neither hot nor cold, I will spit you out of My mouth.*
>
> —Rev. 3:15–16

Many of us have heard this passage, and it's typically explained something like this: "God doesn't want you to follow Him in some areas of your life and disobey Him in others. He would rather you simply pick one—either be completely committed to following Him (i.e., hot) or walk away from Him completely and live like the world (i.e., cold). After all, if you're trying to follow Him and live like the world at the same time, you're neither hot nor cold— you're lukewarm. And God would rather you walk away from Him completely (i.e., be cold) than be lukewarm because lukewarm religion makes Him want to vomit."

On the surface, this sounds really solid, right? It's almost as if God is drawing a line in the sand—we can either stand with Him or stand against Him, but we must choose one or the other. However, there's one problem. We're missing one very important piece of context that completely changes the way we understand this passage.

The Church That Made God Gag

The words in Revelation 3:15–16 were written to the Christians in the city of

Laodicea (see verse 14), which was located in modern-day Turkey. Laodicea was situated near the well-known cities of Hierapolis and Colossae, which were both renowned for their water supplies. Hierapolis had a hot spring that produced water often used for medicinal purposes, and Colossae was located near a cold spring that supplied fresh, cool drinking water to the region.

Laodicea was a city without its own fresh water supply, so the people engineered and constructed an impressive aqueduct system that piped the hot water from Hierapolis and the cold water from Colossae into the city so they could provide their respective benefits to the community.

However, by the time the hot water from Hierapolis and the cold water from Colossae reached the city of Laodicea, both water supplies had become lukewarm. So the water from Hierapolis wasn't hot enough to be useful for medicinal purposes, and the water from Colossae wasn't cold enough to be useful for drinking. In fact, Laodicea's drinking water was so lukewarm and nauseating that instead of swallowing it, they wanted to spit it out—just like Jesus mentions in verse 16.

With this context in mind, we now have a new understanding of Revelation 3:15–16 because we now know that the references to hot and cold are both references to something *good*. In this case, both hot and cold are good because they represent water that would have been useful for something tangible, whether it's for drinking or medicinal purposes. And that's the real point that Jesus is trying to make.

Jesus is telling the Christians of Laodicea that they aren't living up to their purpose. Both the hot and cold water were piped into the city for a reason, but when the water arrived and was lukewarm, it was no longer useful for the purposes it had been brought in for. It was neither healing nor refreshing. And in the same way, the Christians of Laodicea weren't living up to the purpose God had called them to. They had been placed in the city of Laodicea for a reason, to show the majesty and glory of King Jesus so all people would be saved. But instead of living up to their purpose, their lives were like poor drinking water—lukewarm, languid, and gross. No wonder Jesus doesn't say one nice thing about this church.[4]

That's a radically different interpretation than what we typically hear, *but it's biblical.* Jesus isn't telling these Christians that He'd prefer them to abandon their faith completely rather than stay lukewarm. He's using an analogy about water that only the people of Laodicea would have understood in this way, and if we hadn't known the context, we would have missed the point.

Let's take a closer look at how we can unearth the historical context of our passage, James 1:21–25. It's as simple as who, where, when, what, and why.

Who?

Like a detective at a crime scene, the first question we want to ask is this: Who was involved? With the passage we're studying, right away we want to start with James, the author. It may surprise you to know that there are several men named James in the New Testament, so which James wrote our letter? What else does the Bible have to say about James? Is there anything else we can learn about him outside the Bible? What can we learn about him that might help us understand why he was prompted to write this letter?

And James isn't the only person we're interested in. For example, who is he writing to? Is it a group of people or a specific person? How does he know them, and how might that help us get a clearer picture of the passage we're studying?

Typically, when I study a passage, these questions lead me to study multiple people's lives in greater depth. If anyone related to my passage is mentioned elsewhere in the Bible, I go to those verses and read about them, which often leads me to flip to even more parts of the Bible, which in turn leads to even more Bible study. At first that may seem tedious, but everything we learn will help us connect the dots later.

To unearth the answers to my questions, I often use trustworthy Bible study websites such as those below. With a little bit of digging, I can understand the author, recipients, and other important characters a little bit better.

Precept Austin – www.preceptaustin.org

Bible Hub – www.biblehub.com

Blue Letter Bible – www.blueletterbible.org

I also intentionally search out and read books about people who were either mentioned in the Bible or historically important during the time of the Bible. For example, my wife and I have invested in numerous biographies about important biblical figures such as King David, Emperor Nero, Queen Esther, Cyrus the Great, Mary Magdalene, and Caesar Augustus, to name only a few. Studying the lives of those who shaped history during the times of the Bible has proved to be tremendously valuable.

As an additional help for you, in Appendix B (Additional Resources for Bible Study), I have listed many of the books and resources I have found helpful in my journey of learning to study the Bible. While it's certainly not a comprehensive list of the resources you can lean on, they will get you started on the right track.

Where?

We also want to consider where the text was centered geographically. For our purposes, it's important to figure out where James and his readers are located. Once again, these answers can be found in resources such as Bible commentaries, Bible surveys, and the Bible study websites mentioned previously. One additional website, BiblePlaces.com (www.bibleplaces.com), provides excellent high-quality photos of biblical lands that will help you visualize the concepts of your passage.

Once I know the key locations of a passage, I typically like to do more research on what that city or region of the world was like. After all, the Bible wasn't written by people who lived in the West during the 21st century like we do, so I have some cultural and historical barriers to overcome if I want to understand the Bible well. Video teachings by Christian leaders such as Ray Vander Laan and books such as *The Lands of the Bible* by John A. Beck have proved to be very helpful in this area.

When?

Next, we want to figure out when James wrote his book of the Bible. For some books of the Bible, we can nail down the date to an exact year, and for others, we can only narrow the time frame down to a span of several years. Regardless, it is always wise to determine as closely as possible the time frame of your book of the Bible. Once again, this information can typically be found in a Bible commentary, a Bible survey, or one of the websites mentioned earlier.

Once we have this information, it's helpful to pause and consider what life was like back then. How did people live? Were any wars or other important events happening during the time period? Who were the political leaders of the day? Did they have any cultural customs or practices that might help us understand our passage?

Depending on which passage of the Bible you are studying, you may want to learn more about the nomadic lifestyle of Jews in Old Testament times, the

Roman Empire under Nero, the Pharisees during the time of Christ, and any number of other things. In particular, one book that has helped my understanding of Bible customs is *The New Manners & Customs of Bible Times* by Ralph Gower.

What?

Next, we want to consider what historical ideas, topics, or events are being mentioned in the surrounding verses. Many books of the Bible were heavily influenced by important events that were taking place during that time in history. Understanding those events may help us understand our passage.

For example, the book of Lamentations was written by the prophet Jeremiah as he watched the Babylonian army conquer the people of God and destroy the city of Jerusalem. That helps us understand why his language and terminology are so despondent. And the book of Joel was written shortly after a locust invasion that God used to call His people to repentance. That helps us understand why God calls his people to repentance multiple times throughout the short book. As a helpful tip, James wrote his letter in response to a key historical event of the New Testament, and that event provides very helpful context for our passage. We'll unpack that even more in the next chapter.

Why?

Once we've discovered the answers to the questions above, there is one final question to ask. Why does all this matter in the story? After all, the goal here is not to discover neat facts related to our Bible verses so we can impress others with our Bible knowledge. Our goal is to use those details to arrive at truth as we humbly and thoroughly study the Word in its context.

When you study a passage of Scripture for the first time, always assume there is context that you need to uncover. Why did the Holy Spirit prompt James to write this letter at this precise time in history? Who was he writing to, and how did he know them? Why did God see fit to include this passage in His Word? What is God trying to teach us, and how should we live differently as a result? Context always has a *why*, and faithful students of the Bible will not rest until they find it. In fact, that's how we're going to close this chapter.

Your Turn

Let's pause to examine the historical context of the passage we're studying. With the questions below as a guide, use the websites listed earlier to examine the historical context of James. As you study, you can take notes in the space provided below.

Take your time with these questions. The goal isn't necessarily that you get all the right answers; it's that you will see the importance of this process and become better equipped to find the historical context of any passage of Scripture, no matter where your Bible studies take you in the future. When you're finished, I'll see you in the next chapter with the answers to these questions and why they matter. May God bless your studies!

Historical Context for James 1:21–25

Who?

Which James wrote the book of James? _____

_____

Where else is he talked about in the Bible? _____

_____

What can we learn about him from these passages? _____

_____

_____

What else is said about him outside the Bible? _____

_____

Who was he writing to? _____

_____

Where?

Where was James when he wrote this letter? _____

_____

Where was his audience, or more importantly, where were they not? _____

_____

When?

When did James write this book? _____

_____

What else was happening during this time period in history? _____

_____

What?

Read the first chapter of James. Which important historical event does James

mention? _____

_____

What can we learn about this event from the Bible and history? _____

_____

_____

Why?

With all this in mind, why do you think James wrote this letter to his

audience? _____

_____

_____

_____

Conclusion

What has your study of the historical context taught you about our passage?

_____

_____

What questions do you still have about our passage? _____

_____

CHAPTER 7

HISTORICAL CONTEXT – PART 2

For whatever was written in earlier times was written for our instruction, so that through perseverance and the encouragement of the Scriptures we might have hope.

—Rom. 15:4

NOW THAT WE'VE seen the importance of historical context, let's examine the historical context of our passage and why it matters. As you'll see, knowing *why* James wrote our passage is just as important as knowing *what* he wrote. Let's dive in and see what God has to teach us.

Who Is James?

Although there are several men named James in the New Testament, most Bible scholars agree that the author of this book was James, the half-brother of Jesus, also known as James the Just.[5] Thankfully, we can use Scripture and church history to piece together the major details of his life. In John 7:5, we see that Christ's brothers did not believe in Him, which means that by the middle of Christ's earthly ministry, James would still have rejected the Lordship of Jesus. However, in Acts 1:14, we find Mary and the brothers of Jesus (presumably including James) devoting themselves to prayer as they awaited the promised Holy Spirit in faith. So although James didn't believe in Christ during much of His earthly ministry, at some point before Acts 1:14, he chose to follow Jesus.

Later in Acts, we find that James was an apostle and the primary pastor of the thriving church in Jerusalem (Acts 12:17; 15:13; 21:18; Gal. 1:19). In fact, according to Acts 15, he was the primary spokesperson for the Jerusalem church at the Jerusalem Council, and his wisdom decisively determined a key doctrinal matter of the church for both Jews and Gentiles moving forward.

We also know from church history that James was later nicknamed James the Just due to his legacy of righteousness. Eusebius gives us the most complete account of his life, saying that James was known to worship and pray in the temple until his knees were hard and worn like a camel's.[6]

James was faithful to Christ even up to his death as a martyr in 62 AD. Eusebius wrote that James was taken to the pinnacle of the temple and given an ultimatum to turn the people away from Jesus or die. When James started preaching about Jesus, the religious leaders rushed in to throw him down from the pinnacle of the temple. James miraculously survived and prayed that God would forgive his killers as they descended upon him. He was stoned and beaten to death by a fuller's club.[7] May we all learn from his godly example.

Who Is James Writing To?

In James 1:1, we read that James is writing "to the twelve tribes who are dispersed abroad." That tells us two important things about James' audience. First, we know that they are Jewish because he mentions that they are from the 12 tribes of Israel. That makes sense because James was the pastor of the church in Jerusalem, and clearly, he is writing to the people he's responsible to pastor. But second, we learn that these Jewish Christians are not in Jerusalem where James is; they've been "dispersed abroad." That begs the question: Why did these Jewish believers leave town?

What Happened to Prompt This Letter?

This is where the Bible helps us by answering its own questions. After a little bit of digging, we find that this is a reference to the events of Acts 7 where Stephen was stoned to death, becoming the first Christian to die for his faith in Jesus. That event sent shockwaves throughout the church in Jerusalem, but things would only get worse. In the first verse of Acts 8, we read this:

> Saul was in hearty agreement with putting him [Stephen] to death. And on that day a great persecution began against the church in Jerusalem, **and they were all scattered** throughout

the regions of Judea and Samaria, except the apostles (bold emphasis added).

—Acts 8:1

Because of Saul's systematic persecution of the Christians in Jerusalem, the people in James' church fled for their safety. They left behind their homes, their communities, their jobs, and their pastor who longed to continue ministering to their souls. And since James could no longer preach to his people, he picked up his pen to write them a letter of encouragement—a letter we know as the book of James.

This context really helps us grasp what James is saying. After all, when James writes, "Consider it all joy, my brethren, when you encounter various trials" (James 1:2), he isn't writing to 21st century Americans who are worried about the stock market or their influence on social media. He's writing to people who have lost everything because of persecution. James doesn't know if he'll ever see these friends again, so he's writing this letter as his final words of pastoral advice to help guide them through the hardships of beginning a new life after fleeing persecution. Truly, when we take time to understand the context, words like these hit home a little deeper.

Where Was James, and Where Was His Audience?

Because of the research we've already done, we know the answer to this question. From Acts 8:1, we see that James, one of the apostles, would have stayed in Jerusalem despite the systematic and deadly persecution being carried out against the Christians. He's likely in Jerusalem when he pens this note to his people. Most of his church members, however, had fled to Judea and Samaria, the nearby regions just outside of Saul's jurisdiction. Those were the territories where James' letter would have been circulated.

Before we move on, we should note the importance of James' audience being dispersed, specifically to Judea and Samaria. When Christ spoke to His disciples before His ascension to heaven, He said to them, "But you will receive power when the Holy Spirit has come upon you; and you shall be My witnesses both in Jerusalem, **and in all Judea and Samaria**, and even to the remotest part of the earth" (bold emphasis added) (Acts 1:8).

Oh, don't miss this one, my friend! The gospel had already permeated Jerusalem, just as Jesus told His disciples it would. By the time we get to Stephen's death in Acts 7, there are well over 5,000 believers in Jerusalem (Acts 4:4) (note that only the men are counted). The church is growing so rapidly that deacons have been appointed to help with the growing responsibilities that have become too much for the apostles to handle alone (Acts 6:1–7).

But due to Saul's persecution, the multitude of Christians in Jerusalem were forced to run for their lives, and they fled to the next two regions Christ had told them about in Acts 1:8. In other words, the "great persecution" (Acts 8:1), the "various trials" (James 1:2), and the hardships that came from them were all part of God's plan for the gospel to spread to new areas, just as Christ had promised. These Christians weren't just *fleeing* for their lives; they were being *sent out* as Christ's witnesses to Judea and Samaria.

Later in Acts, we see that they fled beyond the regions of Judea and Samaria to remote places such as Phoenicia, Cyprus, and Antioch (Acts 11:19–26). Truly God used their trials for the spread of the gospel across the nations. No wonder James could encourage his readers to count their trials as joy. And perhaps seeing how God used their trials for good can help us count our trials as joy also.

When Did James Write This Letter?

Now that we've nailed down one of the big events that prompted James to write this letter, it shouldn't be difficult to figure out approximately when it was written. After scanning numerous commentaries (I'll share more about commentaries in Chapter 10), I've seen Bible scholars suggest dates anywhere from 40–62 AD, which is the year of James' death. Most commentators suggest a date somewhere in the late 40s AD, which gives us an even more precise estimate.[8] Regardless of the exact year, we do know that James was one of the very first—if not the first—New Testament books to be written.

Why Did James Write Our Specific Passage?

Finally, with all of this in mind, why would James write the verses we're examining together in this book? We know that James is writing to his congregants of the Jerusalem church because they've been scattered abroad by persecution. The persecution had become so great that they left behind their homes, their communities, their church, and everything they had known. However, despite all they left behind, there was at least one thing they were able to take with them—the Word of God. So in James 1:21–25, James encourages his congregants to hear the Word well and prove themselves doers of the Word as they live on mission as witnesses of Christ in Judea and Samaria.

Devote Yourself to Understanding Context

The more you study the Bible, the more historical context you'll arm yourself with. Let me encourage you to look at this like filling out a Sudoku puzzle. At first, there will be quite a few gaps in your understanding of the history of Scripture. But the more you study the Bible, the more you'll fill in those gaps, which in turn makes it easier to fill in the rest of the puzzle as well. Keep devoting yourself to the Scriptures even if you aren't seeing the immediate, tangible results you are looking for. Years from now, your Bible study will yield great results. With that in mind, let's move to another important type of context that you'll want to consider when studying the Bible—the literary context.

CHAPTER 8

LITERARY CONTEXT

For where two or three have gathered together in My name, I am there in their midst.

—Matt. 18:20

HISTORICAL CONTEXT ISN'T the only kind of context we need to search for as we study the Bible. Above is a verse that is often misinterpreted and used in ways that have unintentionally yet deeply hurt the body of Christ. Here's how it's typically explained: This verse is about prayer, and it highlights the importance of Christians praying together in unity because wherever there are two or three (or even more) Christians praying together in unity, Jesus is there with them in their midst.

On the surface, this seems like a wonderful promise. If I want to have Christ's presence in my midst, all I need to do is gather together a few Christian friends and start praying. Then the presence of Jesus will fill the room. It makes sense that this verse is often quoted in prayer meetings and Bible studies as proof that Jesus is with His people when they pray together.

But what about the shut-ins who have no one to pray with them throughout the day? What about those who are alone in prison for following Jesus in countries where it is illegal and even dangerous to be a Christian? What about those who have been forsaken by friends and family because they're following Jesus? If they have no one to pray with, is Jesus not in their midst? Is He not with them in their suffering simply because they weren't able to gather with "two or three"?

All of a sudden, this interpretation is leaving a bad taste in my mouth, kind of like lukewarm water. The reality is that Jesus's presence is always with His followers because He's promised never to leave or forsake us (Heb. 13:5). And in the Sermon on the Mount, Jesus actually encourages us to pray in secret, away from people and alone with the Father (Matt. 6:5–6), which seems to contradict this explanation in Matthew 18:20. The Father hears and answers our prayers on the basis of His Son in whose name we pray rather than on the basis of how many people are sitting in the room with us (John 16:23).

Literary Context

Just as we can learn a lot from studying a passage's historical setting, we can also learn a lot by checking the surrounding verses for context. For example, let's take a look at Matthew 18:20 in light of the verses that come before it. As you examine the whole passage, look for a major theme that might help us understand what Jesus is really teaching His disciples.

> *If your brother sins, go and show him his fault in private; if he listens to you, you have won your brother. But if he does not listen to you, take one or two more with you, so that* BY THE MOUTH OF TWO OR THREE WITNESSES EVERY FACT MAY BE CONFIRMED. *If he refuses to listen to them, tell it to the church; and if he refuses to listen even to the church, let him be to you as a Gentile and a tax collector. Truly I say to you, whatever you bind on earth shall have been bound in heaven; and whatever you loose on earth shall have been loosed in heaven.*
>
> *Again I say to you, that if two of you agree on earth about anything that they may ask, it shall be done for them by My Father who is in heaven. For where two or three have gathered together in My name, I am there in their midst.*
>
> —Matt. 18:15–20

After examining these verses, it becomes clear that Jesus is actually teaching His disciples about church discipline, and the statements He makes about prayer are made only in the context of this larger conversation. But how do we make sense of this? Let's look at Christ's teachings on church discipline first and see if that context clarifies the meaning of our verses.

Church Discipline and Prayer

Christ is saying that if a brother or sister in the church wanders into sin and we see that sinfulness taking root in their lives, we are to lovingly and prayerfully confront them in order to see them restored in their relationship with God and the rest of the church. But if the brother or sister in sin doesn't take the conversation well and refuses to turn from their sin, Jesus tells us to persevere in love by taking along one or two others from the church (two or three people in total) to act as witnesses to the conversation.

Finally, if that conversation does not go well and the brother or sister in sin refuses to humbly repent of their sins, the final confrontation is to happen in front of the entire church. If that brother or sister in sin refuses to listen to the loving rebuke of their entire church, they are to be treated as if they aren't really part of the family of God (i.e., a Gentile or tax collector) because one of the traits of a Christian is that when we do fall into sin, we are quick to humble ourselves before God in repentance.

But what does all this have to do with two or three people gathering together in Jesus's name? And what do Jesus's teachings on church discipline have to do with prayer?

This is where context is so important. After analyzing the surrounding verses, we see one other time that Jesus mentions two or three people—when two or three go to confront the brother or sister in sin.

Don't miss the beauty of Christ's promise to us. He's not promising His presence because we've got enough people in the room to make it worth His time; He's promising His presence because of the tense and difficult situation that church discipline can often lead to. I can remember one such conversation that I was part of early in my ministry, and I didn't sleep well for days leading up to the conversation. I was nervous, over-analyzing every scenario that might happen and how I should respond to what was said. I didn't know what to expect, so I simply remember hoping and praying that the conversation would be taken better than I thought it would. After the conversation went poorly, I remember thinking to myself, "No wonder many churches don't practice church discipline anymore. This is hard!" And that's the reason Christ makes this promise. David Platt's explanation hits the mark.

Remember the context. Jesus has just finished talking about when two or three confront a brother in sin, and Jesus is saying, "Know this: When you gather together in unison to confront sin in the church, you have the full support of the Father in heaven in what you're doing." Jesus knows this church discipline thing is not easy. He knows we will be tempted to shy away from it and not carry it out, so He encourages us here. When two or three people see unrepentant sin in a brother or sister and are caring enough to address it, then know that the Father in heaven is ready to provide you with everything you need to address it. Let's pray according to His promise, and let's be confident in His presence.[9]

Every time we study the Word, we must consider the literary context; otherwise, we are likely to misinterpret and misapply passages such as Matthew 18:20.

The Literary Context for Our Passage

The words of James 1:21–25 were not written in isolation, so we must consider the passages around our passage to get a better idea of what the Holy Spirit is trying to communicate to us. Before continuing, let's get the literary context for our passage by reading the entire first chapter of James.

What are the main things James seems passionate about getting across to his readers? Are there any words or phrases that he repeats multiple times? Is our passage part of a larger conversation that we need to be aware of? Does what we're seeing make sense in light of the historical context we saw in the last chapter? As you read, use the following pages to take note of anything that sticks out to you. When you're finished, I'll see you in the next chapter.

James 1

James, a bond-servant of God and of the Lord Jesus Christ,

To the twelve tribes who are dispersed abroad: Greetings.

Consider it all joy, my brethren, when you encounter various trials, knowing that the testing of your faith produces endurance. And let endurance have its perfect result, so that you may be perfect and complete, lacking in nothing.

56

But if any of you lacks wisdom, let him ask of God, who gives to all generously and without reproach, and it will be given to him. But he must ask in faith without any doubting, for the one who doubts is like the surf of the sea, driven and tossed by the wind. For that man ought not to expect that he will receive anything from the Lord, being *a double-minded man, unstable in all his ways.*

But the brother of humble circumstances is to glory in his high position; and the rich man is to glory *in his humiliation, because like flowering grass he will pass away. For the sun rises with a scorching wind and withers the grass; and its flower falls off and the beauty of its appearance is destroyed; so too the rich man in the midst of his pursuits will fade away.*

Blessed is a man who perseveres under trial; for once he has been approved, he will receive the crown of life which the Lord *has promised to those who love Him. Let no one say when he is tempted, "I am being tempted by God"; for God cannot be tempted by evil, and He Himself does not tempt anyone. But each one is tempted when he is carried away and enticed by his own lust. Then when lust has conceived, it gives birth to sin; and when sin is accomplished, it brings forth death. Do not be deceived, my beloved brethren. Every good thing given and every perfect gift is from above, coming down from the Father of lights, with whom there is no variation or shifting shadow. In the exercise of His will He brought us forth by the word of truth, so that we would be a kind of first fruits among His creatures.*

This you know, my beloved brethren. But everyone must be quick to hear, slow to speak and *slow to anger; for the anger of man does not achieve the righteousness of God. Therefore, putting aside all filthiness and* all *that remains of wickedness, in humility receive the word implanted, which is able to save your souls. But prove yourselves doers of the word, and not merely hearers who delude themselves. For if anyone is a hearer of the word and not a doer, he is like a man who looks at his natural face in a mirror; for once he has looked at himself and gone away, he has immediately forgotten what kind of person he was. But one who looks intently at the perfect law, the law of liberty, and abides by it, not having become a forgetful hearer but an effectual doer, this man will be blessed in what he does.*

If anyone thinks himself to be religious, and yet does not bridle his tongue but deceives his own heart, this man's religion is worthless. Pure and undefiled religion in the sight of our God and Father is this: to visit orphans and widows in their distress, and to keep oneself unstained by the world.

CHAPTER 9

IMPORTANT WORDS AND PHRASES

Your testimonies are righteous forever;
Give me understanding that I may live.

—Ps. 119:144

NOW THAT WE understand the historical and literary context of our passage, it's time to examine the specific words James used to communicate God's truth. Languages are composed of thousands of words, each with its own specific, precise definition. So why did the Holy Spirit direct James to use the exact words he used to write our passage? What do those words mean in the original language James wrote in? And which words are most important to understand our passage?

Although every word of Scripture is *inspired* by God, not every word carries the same level of *importance* when it comes to understanding a particular passage. To be clear, I'm not saying that there are *unimportant* words in Scripture; however, some words carry an *even greater* weight of importance. Thus, interpreting the passage well requires us to know the meanings of the words. They are typically referred to as *keywords*. Let's examine the types of keywords you'll come across as you study the Bible.

Verbs

Verbs are the backbone of sentence structure because they tell us what activity or change is happening in a passage. Because verbs are where the action is, they're the most common type of keyword in the Bible. Below are some examples of verbs in Scripture.

*But God, **being** rich in mercy, because of His great love with which He **loved** us, even when we **were** dead in our transgressions, **made** us alive together with Christ (by grace you have been saved), and **raised** us up with Him, and **seated** us with Him in the heavenly places in Christ Jesus, so that in the ages to come He **might show** the surpassing riches of His grace in kindness toward us in Christ Jesus. For by grace you **have been saved** through faith; and that not of yourselves,* it **is** *the gift of God* (bold emphasis added).

—Eph. 2:4–8

*For He **rescued** us from the domain of darkness, and **transferred** us to the kingdom of His beloved Son, in whom we **have** redemption, the forgiveness of sins* (bold emphasis added).

—Col. 1:13–14

Commands

Just as verbs are the backbone of sentence structure, commands are the backbone of biblical instruction. Through commands, God communicates how we are to follow in the example of our Savior, Jesus. Below are a few examples of commands in the Bible.

*I solemnly charge you in the presence of God and of Christ Jesus, who is to judge the living and the dead, and by His appearing and His kingdom: **preach** the word; **be ready** in season and out of season; **reprove**, **rebuke**, **exhort**, with great patience and instruction* (bold emphasis added).

—2 Tim. 4:1–2

*Rejoice **always**; **pray** without ceasing; in everything **give** thanks; for this is God's will for you in Christ Jesus. **Do not quench** the Spirit; **do not despise** prophetic utterances. But **examine** everything carefully; **hold fast** to that which is good; **abstain** from every form of evil* (bold emphasis added).

—1 Thess. 5:16–22

Absolute Language

Absolute language refers to wording that leaves no room for exceptions. Through absolute language, God communicates truths so strongly that we can stand on them without reservation. To find absolute language, simply keep a lookout for words such as *never, all, none, forever,* and *always.* Below are a few verses that have absolute language.

> *I establish My covenant with you; and all flesh shall* **never again** *be cut off by the water of the flood,* **neither shall there again** *be a flood to destroy the earth* (bold emphasis added).
> —Gen. 9:11

> **All** *that the Father gives Me will come to Me, and the one who comes to Me I will* **certainly not** *cast out* (bold emphasis added).
> —John 6:37

> *For* **all** *have sinned and fall short of the glory of God* (bold emphasis added).
> —Rom. 3:23

> *And I heard a loud voice from the throne, saying, "Behold, the tabernacle of God is among men, and He will dwell among them, and they shall be His people, and God Himself will be among them, and He will wipe away* **every** *tear from their eyes; and there will* **no longer** *be any death; there will* **no longer** *be any mourning, or crying, or pain; the first things have passed away."* (bold emphasis added)
> —Rev. 21:3–4

Connecting Words

Connecting words will connect a verse or passage with the one directly before it, using words such as *therefore, so then,* and *so that.* Both the Psalms and Proverbs use connecting words frequently, but my favorite connecting word—*therefore*—is found in Romans 8:1: "**Therefore** there is now no condemnation for those who are in Christ Jesus" (bold emphasis added).

The word *therefore* connects Paul's statement in Romans 8:1 with the end of Romans 7 where Paul describes his overwhelming and exasperating battle with the sinful flesh. As his frustration reaches a sort of crescendo, he writes, "Wretched man that I am! Who will set me free from the body of this death?" (Rom. 7:24).

Paul is at the end of his spiritual rope. He's been trying to overcome his sinful tendencies and live fully for Jesus, but he cannot overcome sinfulness in his own power. Then, at the height of his frustration, Paul finally looks to Christ. That is when he finds victory, which gives me great hope that as I look to Christ alone, I will also find victory over the sinful tendencies within me. Read the last two verses of Romans 7 and then the first verse of Romans 8 to see how powerful Paul's turn to Christ was in that moment.

> *Wretched man that I am! Who will set me free from the body of this death? Thanks be to God through Jesus Christ our Lord! So then, on the one hand I myself with my mind am serving the law of God, but on the other, with my flesh the law of sin. **Therefore** there is now no condemnation for those who are in Christ Jesus* (bold emphasis added).
>
> —Rom. 7:25—8:1

Contrasting Words

Contrasting words are used to compare and contrast two opposing ideas in order to make a spiritual point. To find contrasting words, simply look for words such as *but* and *yet*. While contrasting language is used throughout Scripture, no one uses it more masterfully than Solomon in the book of Proverbs. Here are a few examples of contrasting words from Proverbs 14.

> *The wise woman builds her house,*
> ***But** the foolish tears it down with her own hands.*
> *He who walks in his uprightness fears the LORD,*
> ***But** he who is devious in his ways despises Him.*
> *In the mouth of the foolish is a rod for his back,*
> ***But** the lips of the wise will protect them.*
> *Where no oxen are, the manger is clean,*
> ***But** much revenue comes by the strength of the ox.*
> *A trustworthy witness will not lie,*

But a false witness utters lies.

A scoffer seeks wisdom and finds *none,*

But knowledge is easy to one who has understanding.

Leave the presence of a fool,

Or you will not discern words of knowledge.

The wisdom of the sensible is to understand his way,

But the foolishness of fools is deceit.

Fools mock at sin,

But among the upright there is good will (bold emphasis added).

—Prov. 14:1–9

Purpose Statements

Purpose statements are words that reveal a reason for what was just said or done in a passage. They are commonly introduced using phrases such as *so that* and *for*. When you see these words, the writer is giving you a reason for something important that has just happened, so be sure to take note. Here are a few examples of purpose statements from 1 Corinthians 9.

*For though I am free from all men, I have made myself a slave to all, **so that** I may win more. To the Jews I became as a Jew, **so that** I might win Jews; to those who are under the Law, as under the Law though not being myself under the Law, **so that** I might win those who are under the Law; to those who are without law, as without law, though not being without the law of God but under the law of Christ, **so that** I might win those who are without law. To the weak I became weak, **that** I might win the weak; I have become all things to all men, **so that** I may by all means save some. I do all things for the sake of the gospel, **so that** I may become a fellow partaker of it* (bold emphasis added).

—1 Cor. 9:19–23

Repeated Words

In addition, it is helpful to mark any words that are repeated multiple times in a passage. Sometimes the word is repeated back-to-back such as when the seraphim exclaim, "**Holy, Holy, Holy**, is the LORD of hosts, the whole earth is full of His glory!" (bold emphasis added) (Isa. 6:3). Usually, a repeated word or phrase is splattered throughout a passage and requires intentional observation to find them.

If your passage uses the same word or phrase multiple times, it will typically jump out at you when you examine the literary context. For example, as you read Revelation 4 and 5, you will see a major emphasis on the word *worthy*, which John repeats many times to point us to the worthiness of Christ our Redeemer (Rev. 4:11; 5:2; 5:4; 5:9; 5:12). And when you study Haggai, you'll notice God frequently exhorts the people to *consider* their ways (Hag. 1:5; 1:7; 2:15; 2:17).

Lists of Related Words

There is no such thing as a random list of words in the Bible. Each list is intentionally designed to build up to a powerful point. So when you see a list of three or more related words, examine it closely. For example, take note of the list Peter uses to encourage us to grow to maturity in the faith, and consider how each character trait builds on the previous one to culminate in the spiritually mature Christian.

> *Now for this very reason also, applying all diligence, in your* **faith** *supply* **moral excellence**, *and in* your **moral excellence**, **knowledge**, *and in* your **knowledge**, **self-control**, *and in* your **self-control**, **perseverance**, *and in* your **perseverance**, **godliness**, *and in* your **godliness**, **brotherly kindness**, *and in* your **brotherly kindness**, **love**. *For if these qualities are yours and are increasing, they render you neither useless nor unfruitful in the true knowledge of our Lord Jesus Christ* (bold emphasis added).
>
> —2 Pet. 1:5–8

Other Important Words

While the types of keywords above will help you uncover most of the keywords in any Bible passage, they are by no means an exhaustive list. So after looking for these types of keywords, I typically sweep my passage one more time, marking any words that might help me understand my passage better. If a word looks important, I want to know what it means.

As a good rule of thumb, even if you're unsure whether a word's meaning will be important or not, take the time to mark it for closer examination. After all, it is worth analyzing every word of a passage because even words that *seem* unimportant could make or break your understanding of that passage. We'll find that to be true of James 1:21–25 in just a few chapters.

Now It's Your Turn

Before we move on, let me encourage you to take some time to circle or highlight every keyword you can find in our passage, taking special care to note keywords whose definitions might be helpful for you to know. Once you're finished, add 10 observations based exclusively on the words you've marked. Do you see any patterns? Are there any repeated words that stand out? Which verbs or commands seem most important, and are there any purpose statements that help you see why James wrote the passage? I took the liberty of writing the first observation to get you started. Take your time filling in the rest, and when you're ready, I'll see you in the next chapter.

> *Therefore, putting aside all filthiness and all that remains of wickedness, in humility receive the word implanted, which is able to save your souls. But prove yourselves doers of the word, and not merely hearers who delude themselves. For if anyone is a hearer of the word and not a doer, he is like a man who looks at his natural face in a mirror; for* once *he has looked at himself and gone away, he has immediately forgotten what kind of person he was. But one who looks intently at the perfect law, the* law *of liberty, and abides by it, not having become a forgetful hearer but an effectual doer, this man will be blessed in what he does.*
>
> —James 1:21–25

1. The word *all* is used twice in verse 21. That is absolute language.

2. _____

3. _____

4. _____

5. _____

6. _____

7. _____

8. _____

9. _____

10. _____

CHAPTER 10

LOOKING UP KEYWORDS – PART 1

I am Your servant, give me understanding,
That I may know Your testimonies.

—Ps. 119:125

NOW THAT WE'VE figured out which words in our passage matter most, we are one massive step closer to understanding our passage. The keywords we marked in the last chapter are now our primary focus as we finish analyzing the Word. However, we have one hurdle remaining. We haven't defined those words.

For example, what does it mean to "put aside all filthiness," and how do we do that? What does James have in mind when he thinks of proving ourselves "doers" of the Word? And if our passage finishes by promising that the doer will be "blessed" in what they do, then what does that blessing look like? At first, this may seem like splitting hairs or over-analyzing, but as you'll see in the next chapter, keyword definitions may be the most important pieces of information you can gather as you study.

Remember that James is writing these words in a different language than you and I are reading them in. And as intentional as Bible translators are, sometimes words and concepts can get lost in translation. However, as we return to the original languages of Scripture, the Word really begins to jump off the page with raw, impactful meanings—and that's our goal in this chapter.

What If I Don't Know Hebrew or Greek?

If the idea of looking up and defining Greek or Hebrew words seems overwhelming, then let me assure you that you do not need to be an expert in the biblical languages to look up keywords. I don't consider myself very well-versed in either Hebrew or Greek, so if I can master looking up keywords, I know you can do it too.

By God's grace, faithful men and women who have been well-trained in the original languages of Scripture have devoted their lives to understanding and defining the words of the Bible. Much of their work is available to us online for free. You simply need to know where to look for the information, and that's what we'll examine in this chapter. First, let's look at the tools you may find beneficial as you study a passage's keywords.

BIBLE STUDY TOOLS

Lexicons and Concordances

The first tools you'll want to use as you look up keywords are lexicons and concordances. Concordances are the most widely used Bible study resource, and they are essentially large keyword dictionaries that are alphabetized for easy lookup. For example, if you're studying Leviticus 16 and you want to know what the word *atonement* means, you can look it up in your concordance and find which Hebrew word is used in the particular verse you're studying. Then, when you look up the corresponding Hebrew word, you can find a basic definition of what it means. The most widely used concordance is *Strong's Concordance*, which is available online for free. However, if you're like me and prefer a physical book to reference as you study, you can also find a *Strong's Concordance* at your local Christian bookstore.

A lexicon is similar to a concordance but begins with the original Hebrew or Greek languages rather than starting with the English word. In addition, a good lexicon will show you the root word of your keyword in its original language, as well as its variations and where they're used in Scripture. For that reason, I prefer to use a lexicon when looking up keywords. It helps you walk away with a more complete understanding of what your keyword means. Again, these are typically available online for free, but if you're looking for a physical copy of your own, I recommend *The Brown-Driver-Briggs Hebrew and English Lexicon* for Old Testament keywords and *Thayer's Greek-English Lexicon of the New Testament: Coded with Strong's Concordance Numbers* for New Testament keywords.

Bible Dictionaries and Surveys

A Bible dictionary gives you a quick overview of the various topics, people, places, and ideas in the Bible. If you're studying Leviticus 16 and have no idea what atonement is, you can look up atonement in your Bible dictionary and get a quick summary of what atonement means and how it's used in the Bible. You can find several great Bible dictionaries for free online, but if you'd like to purchase one for your study time, I typically recommend *The Baker Illustrated Bible Background Commentary* by J. Scott Duvall and J. Daniel Hays.

Bible surveys are also helpful for understanding the big story of Scripture and how each book of the Bible fits into that narrative. Bible surveys are typically focused specifically on either the Old Testament or the New Testament and provide historical and literary context similar to what we did in Chapters 6–8 of this book. You can find much of this information for free on sites such as Precept Austin or Bible Hub; however, if you'd like to purchase a Bible survey of your own, I'd encourage you to get *The Promise and the Blessing* by Michael A. Harbin. It covers both the Old and New Testaments in one Bible survey and does a tremendous job of outlining what you need to know as you study each book of the Bible. In addition, the video resources provided by *Bible Project* are very good at showing how each book of the Bible fits into the overall story of Scripture. Time spent on this website would be very beneficial as you begin studying a new book of the Bible.

Bible Atlases

When your passage refers to a geographic location, a Bible atlas will help you understand the history, culture, and even customs of that particular place. A good Bible atlas contains maps, pictures, and charts of the lands of the Bible, along with important information about the time period of Scripture. This context may prove invaluable when it comes to making sense of the passages you're studying. Many excellent Bible atlas resources are available online for free, but if you'd like a physical Bible atlas to look at as you study, I recommend both the *Zondervan Atlas of the Bible* by Carl G. Rasmussen and *The New Moody Atlas of the Bible* by Barry J. Beitzel.

Commentaries

Finally, commentaries can help you understand what a keyword means in the context of its passage. Keyword definitions may vary dramatically depending on the context (especially Hebrew keywords), so if you find yourself confused, a good commentary might help guide you through how to make sense of your word in light of the passage it was written in. There are several excellent commentary sets available online as well as for purchase. If you'd like to have commentaries on hand as you study, I recommend purchasing the *New International Commentary on the Old Testament (NICOT)* and the *New International Commentary on the New Testament (NICNT)*. If you would like to do your own research on commentaries before making a purchase, then Best Commentaries (bestcommentaries.com) will be your new best friend.

The Tools We'll Be Using for Our Study

For our keyword studies, we'll use the best free online resources, so you don't need to spend money to follow along and look up keywords for yourself. In this chapter, we'll be using two main sources—Bible Hub and Precept Austin—that are described in detail for you on the next few pages. Both of these resources have contributed much to my own spiritual growth, and I hope that with time and practice, you will derive as much spiritual benefit from them as I have.

Bible Hub Lexicon

Bible Hub is an excellent online Bible study website full of free resources and tools that could keep you busy for a lifetime. I'm deeply indebted to Bible Hub for much of my own spiritual growth. The site has also proved helpful for many others. For the sake of our keyword lookups, we'll be using Bible Hub Lexicon (https://biblehub.com/lexicon/james/1-21.htm). Simply put the link into your web browser, and when you get there, you should see something similar to the screenshot below.

◀ **James 1:21** ▶

NASB Lexicon

NASB ©	Greek	Strong's	Origin
Therefore,	διὸ (dio)	1352 wherefore, on which account	from dia and hos.
putting aside	ἀποθέμενοι (apothemenoi)	659 to put off, lay aside	from apo and tithēmi
all	πᾶσαν (pasan)	3956 all, every	a prim. word
filthiness	ῥυπαρίαν (ruparian)	4507b fig. filthiness	from rhuparos
and [all] that remains	περισσείαν (perisseian)	4050 superfluity	from perisseuō
of wickedness,	κακίας (kakias)	2549 wickedness	from kakos
in humility	πραΰτητι (prautēti)	4240 gentleness	from praus

Bible Hub Lexicon for James 1:21

As you can see, this page shows you the English words of our verse on the left (column 1), the corresponding Greek word (column 2), its *Strong's Concordance* number and definition (column 3), and the origin of the word (column 4).

In this chapter, we'll be looking up the keywords *putting aside*. To take a closer look at what they mean, simply click on the blue number 659, which is *Strong's* number for that Greek word. That should take you to a page that looks similar to the screenshot below. From there, you can view a wealth of information about the Greek word for *putting aside*, including its definition, usages, and other ways it is translated in the Bible. Take some time to review this page before we dive into our next online resource.

◀ 659. apotithémi ▶

Strong's Concordance

apotithémi: to put off, lay aside
Original Word: ἀποτίθημι
Part of Speech: Verb
Transliteration: apotithémi
Phonetic Spelling: (ap-ot-eeth'-ay-mee)
Definition: to put off, lay aside
Usage: I lay off or aside, renounce, stow away, put.

NAS Exhaustive Concordance

Word Origin
from apo and tithémi
Definition
to put off, lay aside

NASB Translation
laid aside (1), lay aside (3), laying aside (1), put (1), put...aside (1), putting aside (2).

Englishman's Concordance

Matthew 14:3 V-AIM-3S
GRK: ἐν φυλακῇ ἀπέθετο διὰ Ἡρῳδιάδα
NAS: he bound *him and put* him in prison
INT: in prison *put [him]* on account of Herodias

Acts 7:58 V-AIM-3P
GRK: οἱ μάρτυρες ἀπέθεντο τὰ ἱμάτια
NAS: [him]; and the witnesses *laid aside* their robes
KJV: the witnesses *laid down* their
INT: the witnesses *laid aside* the garments

Romans 13:12 V-ASM-1P
GRK: ἡμέρα ἤγγικεν ἀποθώμεθα οὖν τὰ
NAS: Therefore *let us lay aside* the deeds
KJV: therefore *cast off* the works
INT: [the] day has drawn near *we should cast off* therefore the

Ephesians 4:22 V-ANM
GRK: ἀποθέσθαι ὑμᾶς κατὰ
NAS: manner of life, *you lay aside* the old
KJV: That ye *put off* concerning the former
INT: *to have put off* you according to

Bible Hub Lexicon for apotithemi

Precept Austin Verse-by-Verse Commentaries

Precept Austin is one of the best and most thorough online commentaries on the Internet (https://www.preceptaustin.org/verse_by_verse). Entirely free to use, this site is another one you could seemingly spend a lifetime on. Its commentaries do a masterful job of translating keywords, and its analyses are remarkably sound. Precept Austin has a commentary for almost every New Testament verse and much of the Old Testament as well. Simply enter the web address below into your browser, and you should see a web page like the following screenshot.

Verse by Verse Commentaries by Book

View Recently Updated Pages

Old Testament:

Genesis	2 Chronicles	Daniel
Exodus	Ezra	Hosea
Leviticus	Nehemiah	Joel
Numbers	Esther	Amos
Deuteronomy	Job	Obadiah
Joshua	Psalms	Jonah
Judges	Proverbs	Micah
Ruth	Ecclesiastes	Nahum
1 Samuel	Song of Solomon	Habakkuk
2 Samuel	Isaiah	Zephaniah
1 Kings	Jeremiah	Haggai
2 Kings	Lamentations	Zechariah
1 Chronicles	Ezekiel	Malachi

Here, you will find an entire library of Precept Austin commentaries. Since we'll be viewing the commentary for James 1:21, simply click on James, and then scroll down to James 1:21 Commentary. That will open a page that looks like the following screenshot.

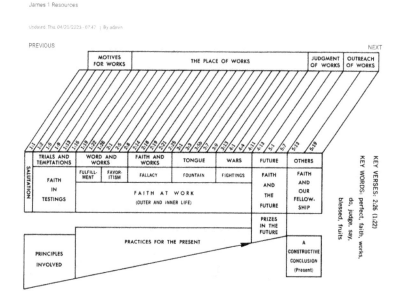

Since we're focused on looking up the Greek word for *putting aside*, scroll down until you see that keyword phrase highlighted in yellow. Take some time to review this information. Next, I'll show you how to make sense of everything you've just read.

BIBLE STUDY TIPS

Looking up keywords can expose you to a mountain of information about a Hebrew or Greek word. So how do you sort through the fluff to figure out what your keyword means and better understand your passage? Let's look at how to make sense of what you'll find as you dig for answers.

First, Look for Literal Definitions

Every Hebrew or Greek word has a literal definition that is best expressed using two or three English words or phrases. For example, let's look up the first keyword of our passage, *putting aside*. After doing some digging on Bible Hub's lexicon site, I noticed that the Greek word literally means "to put off or lay aside something" (see below).

Strong's Concordance

apotithémi: to put off, lay aside
Original Word: ἀποτίθημι
Part of Speech: Verb
Transliteration: apotithémi
Phonetic Spelling: (ap-ot-eeth'-ay-mee)

Definition: to put off, lay aside
Usage: I lay off or aside, renounce, stow away, put.

Precept Austin makes the literal definition even clearer, describing it as "to put or take something away from its normal location and thus to put it out of the way (way out of the way!)."

Putting aside (659) (apotithemi from **apo** = away from, marker of dissociation, implying a rupture from a former association, separation, departure, cessation, any separation of one thing from another by which the union or fellowship of the two is destroyed + **tithemi** = put, place) means literally to put or take something away from its normal location and thus to put it out of the way (way out of the way!). It was used **literally** of runners who participated in the Olympic games who stripped off and cast aside their clothes and then ran almost completely naked in the stadium.

Second, Look for Word Pictures

One of the most important things to understand about Hebrew and Greek is that they are both graphic languages, which means that many of our keywords will have a picture or idea associated with them. These word pictures will help us visualize what James is saying in a way that makes his words easier to understand and remember.

For example, let's return to our first keyword, *putting aside*. When we go to Precept Austin, we find that the word was used to refer to "runners who participated in the Olympic Games who stripped off and cast aside their clothes and then ran almost completely naked in the stadium." As a sort of word picture, this particular keyword visualizes taking off your clothes and casting them aside before running a race, a practice often used in the ancient Olympic Games.

However, as we read further on Precept Austin's commentary for James 1:21, we find an additional word picture that might be of benefit to us.

Putting aside is an aorist participle (in English usually identified by a word that ends in "-ing") which calls for this putting aside to be accomplished as an effective action, by a definite break with the things mentioned. It is the condition that must be fulfilled in order to facilitate the ready reception of the Word as discussed below. James use of the aorist tense here stresses the importance of a once for all putting off of sin prior to receiving God's Word. James says our filthy, wicked vices are likened to soiled garments which are to be set aside once for all.

Here we find that the word was also used to picture soiled and filthy garments, "which are to be set aside once for all." The word picture is becoming clear. We're being told to put aside something soiled and filthy like a filthy old shirt that is no longer useful to wear.

Third, Look for Specific Information about How the Keyword Is Used in Your Passage

This is where our technical knowledge of the biblical languages will certainly fail us if not for the wonderful help available to us in concordances and lexicons. You see, one biblical keyword may be used in different contexts and with different emphases, depending on the passage and the situation. Sometimes a particular word carries a tone to it that we would miss if not for some of the resources we have at our disposal.

In the case of our keyword, Precept Austin's commentary on James 1:21 once again proves helpful to us. We find that this particular use of our word is an aorist participle, which signifies doing something once and for all. It is an "effective action, by a definite break with the things mentioned." In other words, James is telling us to "put aside all filthiness and all that remains of wickedness" *and never return to pick it up again.* This is no half-hearted repentance that begs for forgiveness one second only to turn around and commit the same evil again a second later. This is a definitive break from the sin that is holding us back from proving ourselves doers of the Word. Knowing this helps us understand that James is writing this verse with a sort of intensity that we might have missed if we hadn't looked up our keyword.

Fourth, Define the Keyword in Light of Your Passage

Finally, we want to return to our passage and define the word in light of what else James is saying. In our specific verse, James is telling us to put aside "all filthiness and all that remains of wickedness." We'll look up more of those words in a minute, which will make our picture even clearer, but for now, we know that the best way to describe our keyword is with the idea of taking off old, dirty clothes and never wearing them again. With this in mind, we can define our word as "to put away or lay something down for good." That's a solid description of what "putting aside" means in our passage.

Now It's Your Turn

This is my favorite part of the Bible study process. Nothing helps me understand a passage more than looking up its keywords. I can't tell you how many times I've looked up a keyword and been blown away at what it means and how it impacts my understanding of the Bible. There are some days when I have to stop looking up keywords because my heart is overflowing with worship, and my mind is processing truths I'd never understood before.

Keywords will prove to be vital when it comes to forming our interpretation of James 1:21–25. So, before you move on to the next chapter, take some time to look up each of the keywords of our passage that are in bold below. You can make notes in the space provided on the next few pages. Once you've examined each word and discovered its meaning, I'll see you in the next chapter where we'll compare notes on what we've found. I pray that the time you spend looking up the keywords of our passage will be helpful to you. May God bless your study!

Therefore, **putting aside** all **filthiness** and *all* that **remains** of **wickedness**, in **humility receive** the **word implanted**, which is **able** to **save** your **souls**. But **prove** yourselves **doers** of the word, and not merely **hearers** who **delude** themselves. For if anyone is a hearer of the word and not a doer, he is like a **man** who **looks** at his **natural face** in a **mirror**; for *once* he **has looked** at himself and **gone away**, he has **immediately forgotten** what kind of person he was. But one who **looks intently** at the **perfect law**, the law of **liberty**, and **abides** by it, not having become a **forgetful** hearer but an **effectual doer**, this man will be **blessed** in what he does (bold emphasis added).

—James 1:21–25

Verse 21

Putting Aside – _____

_____

Filthiness – _____

_____

Remains – _____

_____

Wickedness – _____

_____

Humility – _____

_____

Receive – _____

_____

Word – _____

_____

Implanted – _____

_____

Able – _____

_____

Save – _____

_____

Souls – _____

_____

Verse 22

Prove – _____

_____

Doers – _____

_____

Hearers – _____

_____

Delude – _____

_____

Verse 23

Man – _____

_____

Looks – _____

_____

Natural face – _____

_____

Mirror – _____

_____

Verse 24

Has looked – _____

_____

Gone away – _____

_____

Immediately – _____

_____

Forgotten – _____

_____

Verse 25

Looks intently – _____

_____

Perfect – _____

_____

Law – _____

_____

Liberty – _____

_____

Abides – _____

_____

Forgetful – _____

_____

Effectual doer – _____

_____

Blessed – _____

_____

CHAPTER 11

LOOKING UP KEYWORDS – PART 2

Open my eyes, that I may behold
Wonderful things from Your law.

—Ps. 119:18

IN THIS CHAPTER, we'll examine each of the keywords of James 1:21–25 in their original language. I'll share summaries and definitions of each Greek word from my own personal studies so you can compare what I have with your notes from the previous chapter.

For the sake of our study, I've limited my research to only free online resources so you can follow along with these keyword studies without spending any money. However, if you're interested in purchasing your own keyword resources that often provide more in-depth analysis, see Appendix B: Bible Study Resources, which will provide you with a list of concordances and lexicons that I recommend.

In Appendix C: Keyword Resources, I've also included references and links to various commentaries, books, and websites that I've used to look up the keywords of our passage. You'll notice that I *never* take only one dictionary or website at its word. I always try to find a minimum of three credible sources to confirm the meaning of a keyword.

Alright, my friend, let's dive into our keywords. As we do, I pray that the Holy Spirit will help us piece together what God is trying to teach us.

Putting Aside – ἀποθέμενοι (apothemenoi)
This Greek word is a compound word made from *apo*, which means "away from," and *titheme*, which means "put, place, or lay down." Combined, these

81

mean "to put away or lay something down away from yourself." It is used nine times in the New Testament, and in most of those verses, we are being exhorted to put away or lay down something sinful and displeasing to God.

The Greek tense of this word requires a once-and-for-all action. In other words, James is telling us to "put aside" our filthiness with no intention of returning to it or picking it up again. The idea here is that those who "put aside" their filthiness with the intent of returning to it later haven't truly repented.

Filthiness – ῥυπαρίαν (rhuparian)

This Greek word literally means "dirt or filth" and refers to the dirt that would soil someone's clothing. It is often used figuratively to refer to moral filthiness. The root word for *rhuparian* is *rhupos*, which is a medical term that referred to an excess buildup of earwax. That buildup would make hearing difficult until it was removed.

Remains – περισσείαν (perisseian)

Perisseian is a noun that means "excess, overflow, surplus, superabundance, or overabundance." It is used three additional times in the New Testament (Rom. 5:17; 2 Cor. 8:2; 2 Cor. 10:15). In these verses, we see "the abundance of grace" that is received by the Christian through the gospel of Christ and the "abundance of joy" that prompted the generosity of the Macedonians despite their poverty and affliction. In the context of our verse, James is saying that the believer needs to put aside their "overabundance" of wickedness before receiving the Word.

Wickedness – κακίας (kakias)

This is the general Greek word for evil and wickedness. It refers not only to evil actions but also to evil thoughts, motives, and attitudes. When combined with the previous word, it carries the idea of an abnormal, unhealthy growth of wickedness in the heart, almost picturing sinfulness as a tumor or a garden weed that stunts the spiritual development of the believer.

Humility – πραΰτητι (prauteti)

This Greek word has no precise English equivalent, but it is typically translated as "meekness, gentleness, or humility." In the context of this verse, it refers to having a humble and teachable spirit. Outside of the Bible, *prauteti* was sometimes used to refer to a horse that had been broken and trained to submit to the direction of its rider.[10] Thus, the idea here is of someone who is eager to be taught by the Word and willing to submit to its direction.

Receive – δέξασθε (dexasthe)

Dexasthe is a Greek verb that literally means "to receive." It pictures joyfully welcoming guests into your home or receiving something given to you by grasping it with your hand. In this verse, we're told to "receive" the Word much like the Bereans did. Listen to Luke's description of these godly people and their eager reception of the Word.

> *Now these [the Bereans] were more noble-minded than those in Thessalonica,* **for they received [dexasthe] the Word with great eagerness,** *examining the Scriptures daily to see whether these things were so* (bold emphasis added).
>
> —Acts 17:11

Amen. May we all receive and welcome the Word with the same humility and eagerness as the Bereans did. And to be clear, this Greek word is a verb, which means that it denotes intentional action. Just as we actively receive guests into our homes, we must also actively receive the Word into our hearts by faith.

Word – λόγον (logon)

Logon literally means "word," and in this context, it is a clear reference to the Word of God. The Word is God's clear communication to us about who He is, how much He loves us, and why He is worthy of all glory, honor, and praise. It is this Word, not another word, that we are to receive with humility and a teachable spirit.

Implanted – ἔμφυτον (emphuton)

This word means "to implant" and literally pictures planting a seed in soil. However, not all implanted seeds bear fruit. The growth of the seed depends on the fertility of the soil. In the same way, the Word implanted in our hearts must be welcomed into receptive soil marked by humility (James 1:21). This imagery reminds us of Christ's parable of the Sower and the seed (Mark 4:1–20).

Able – δυνάμενον (dunamenon)

The word for "able" is *dunamenon*, from which our English word *dynamite* was later formed. It is used 210 times in the New Testament and means "to have power or the capacity to do something; to be able." Just as dynamite has the power and ability to blast away rock or clear debris, the Word has the power and ability to save our souls and the souls of those around us who desperately need salvation. This echoes Peter's first epistle.

> *For you have been born again not of seed which is perishable but imperishable, that is, through the living and enduring word of God.*
>
> —1 Pet. 1:23

Just pause for a moment to consider the massive weight of that statement. How important it is that we receive this Word in humility. Our very souls depend on it!

Save – σῶσαι (sosai)

What a word this is! *Sosai* literally means "to deliver out of danger and into safety." It is used to refer to God rescuing believers from the power and penalty of sin and into safety by virtue of our union with Jesus Christ, His Son. This Greek word also functions as the root word for other important words in the Bible such as *Savior* and *salvation*. According to James, God's primary means of drawing people to Christ for salvation is through His Word. May we receive it gladly and with great humility and urge others to do the same.

Souls – ψυχὰς (psuchas)

This Greek word literally means "to breathe or blow" and refers to the human soul. Your soul is the very core of your being. It is more than merely your body or your mind. It is *you*. Your soul is immortal and thus will be subject to either God's wrath or God's salvation for all eternity. Could anything be more important than the salvation of your soul? God, help us not to take our soul lightly when You have valued it so highly.

Prove – Γίνεσθε (ginesthe)

The Greek word for *prove* means "to come into being or to become" and pictures transitioning from one state to another, just as the caterpillar becomes a butterfly. In this verse, the stress is on continually being doers of the Word rather than hearers. In other words, the transition James calls for is to be permanent. Just as the caterpillar becomes a butterfly once and for all, let us become doers who never go back to merely hearing the Word.

Doers – ποιηταὶ (poietai)

This word refers to "a performer, actor, author, or poet" and pictures one who performs as directed—in this case, one who performs the Word by doing what it says. It's as if James pictures us as actors who have for our script the very Word of God. The Bible is not merely meant to be heard; it is meant to be acted upon continually.

Hearers – ἀκροαταὶ (akroatai)

Akroatai is a very basic Greek word that refers to "a hearer or listener." It was often used in Greek culture of a person who attended a lecture but failed to follow the lecturer's advice and wise counsel. In this context, James uses it to refer to one who hears the Word and yet fails to live in light of its teachings.

Delude – παραλογιζόμενοι (paralogizomenoi)

This is a compound word taken from *para*, which means "contrary to or against," and *logizemai*, which means "reason." Combined, they refer to someone who has reasoned contrary to the truth about a matter and has ultimately miscalculated. Like a sailor who miscalculates the stars by which they're sailing, these individuals go in the wrong direction and end up at the wrong destination.

Oh, this is important, my friend. James is telling us that the person who settles for merely hearing the Word has made a major miscalculation. The hearer acts contrary to reason because they have reasoned contrary to the truth of the Word.

Man – ἀνδρὶ (andri)

While there are Greek words that can be used to refer to humanity in general, this Greek word specifically means "a male." Depending on the context, it can be used to refer to a man, husband, father, brother, or son, although here it seems to refer simply to a man.

Looks – κατανοοῦντι (katanoounti)

This keyword is a compound word formed from *kata*, which means "down" and adds to the intensity of a word, and *noeo*, which means "to perceive, see, or think." Combined, they picture setting the mind on something until it is perceived or clearly understood. The point here is that this man in James' mirror analogy doesn't take a passing glance at the mirror. He lingers long enough to clearly perceive his "natural face."

Natural Face – γενέσεως πρόσωπον (geneseos prosopon)

This is really two Greek keywords that combine to form one phrase. *Geneseos* is where we get our English word *genesis* and refers to a person's beginning or birth. *Prosopon* is a compound word made up of *pros* and *ops*, which combine to mean "one's physical face." When you put these words together, you get "the face one has had from the beginning or from their birth."

Mirror – ἐσόπτρῳ (esoptro)

Esoptro refers to an object for looking into, particularly a mirror. In the New Testament era, mirrors were not made of glass but rather of heavily polished bronze, silver, or other precious metals. You would have to stare into it to gain an accurate picture of your natural face. The mirror would reveal what a person truly looked like, giving them an opportunity to make changes to their appearance, if necessary.

Has Looked – κατανοοῦντι (katanoounti)

This is the same compound word we saw in the previous verse under "looks." It refers to setting the mind on something until it is perceived or clearly understood.

Gone Away – ἀπελήλυθεν (apelēluthen)

Here we find yet another compound word. This one is formed by combining *apo*, which means "away from," and *erchomai*, which means "to come or go." In this context, we know it is referring to the man walking away from the mirror after clearly perceiving his reflection.

Immediately – εὐθέως (eutheos)

This is a basic Greek word that literally means "immediately, at once, directly, or right away." Within the context of our passage, James is saying that when the man walks away from the mirror, he immediately forgets what he perceived when he looked in the mirror.

Forgotten – ἐπελάθετο (epelatheto)

This is another compound word formed from *epi*, which means "on or upon," and adds intensity to the compound word, and *lanthano*, which means "to be hidden, concealed, or go unnoticed." When combined, these words refer to something that is neglected and then completely forgotten.

As a result, we know that this forgetfulness does not stem from a poor memory but from poor priorities. Both the hearer and the man in the mirror are forgetful because they don't think what they've seen is important enough to remember, and according to James, that is a terrible miscalculation.

Looks Intently – παρακύψας (parakupsas)

Here we find another compound keyword formed from *para* and *kupto*, which mean "beside or close to" and "bend forward, stoop down," respectively. Combined, they refer to bending down and closely inspecting something of great importance. The one who "looks intently" is not easily distracted or interrupted because their whole focus is on examining something that has captivated their attention. Whenever I see this word in Scripture, I can't help but picture a scientist peering intently through their microscope at something of great interest.

As a side note, this word is very important for us because it marks our first keyword difference between the hearer and the doer. James has now used two words to describe how these men *look* in the mirror. Clearly, they look in the mirror differently because they place a different level of *importance* on the mirror and what it has to show them. We'll want to keep this in mind as we interpret our passage in the next chapter.

Perfect – τέλειον (teleion)

Teleion literally means "perfect, complete, and mature" and refers to something that has reached its intended goal. James applies this perfection to the law, meaning that the law is a reflection of God's own holy perfection. The law of God cannot be improved upon nor is it lacking in any way.

Law – νόμον (nomon)

This Greek word means "law, decree, or custom" and is used frequently in the New Testament to refer to the divine laws of God that are perfect in nature (see previous keyword) and that sets us at liberty from sin and death (see next keyword). David makes a similar statement about the law of God in Psalm 19.

> *The law of the LORD is perfect, restoring the soul;*
> *The testimony of the LORD is sure, making wise the simple.*
> *The precepts of the LORD are right, rejoicing the heart;*
> *The commandment of the LORD is pure, enlightening the eyes.*
> *The fear of the LORD is clean, enduring forever;*
> *The judgments of the LORD are true; they are righteous altogether.*
> *They are more desirable than gold, yes, than much fine gold;*
> *Sweeter also than honey and the drippings of the honeycomb.*
> *Moreover, by them Your servant is warned;*
> *In keeping them there is great reward.*
>
> Ps. 19:7–11

Liberty – ἐλευθερίας (eleutherias)

Eleutherias literally means "freedom or liberty" and pictures being unshackled and set free from bondage. It is used 11 times in the New Testament, and each time it carries the idea of being set free—having freedom of movement and ability that you had not previously possessed.

Don't miss what James is saying through these keywords. The law is not merely a set of rules and obligations for you to follow. It is joy and freedom for your soul. God's Word is perfect and able to set you free from the shackles of sin so you no longer have to serve your sinful desires. The law grants you freedom, not to live for yourself but to live fully for Christ. Through His perfect and liberating Word, God can save you (James 1:21) and set you free to walk in the joy that comes from a life of obedience—the life of a doer.

Abides – παραμείνας (parameinas)

This Greek word means "to remain beside or near" and carries the idea of persevering in what you are doing. It is used four times in the New Testament, and here it seems to convey the meaning of dwelling in front of the mirror continuously, certainly long after the hearers have left and forgotten their appearance.

To abide in the perfect law of liberty like this implies a single-minded focus. The doer is often in the Word and is not easily distracted and drawn away from it like the hearer.

Forgetful – ἐπιλησμονῆς (epilesmones)

This keyword is very similar to the word *forgotten*, which we have already examined. It means "to neglect, forget, or fail to notice." In the context of our passage, this forgetfulness is ascribed to the hearer but not the doer. It is yet another difference between these two men who we would do well to keep in mind moving forward.

Effectual Doer – ἔργου ποιητής (ergou poietes)

In contrast to the "forgetful hearer," James describes the "effectual doer." This phrase is formed from two keywords. The word for *doer* is the same word that we saw previously, which means "a performer, actor, author, or poet" and pictures one who carries out or performs as directed—in this case, one who performs the Word by doing what it says.

The Greek word for *effectual* is *ergou* and literally means "work." It carries the idea of swift, intense action, meaning that the doer is not slow, lazy, or nonchalant about performing the Word. Being a doer of the Word is their life's work, and they do it with all their might.

Blessed – μακάριος (makarios)

Makarios means "large, happy, blessed, or even to be envied." The idea behind this word is that when God blesses an individual, their lives are enlarged, which results in such great joy that others might become envious of the joy they possess. *Makarios* was originally used by the Greeks to refer to their gods who didn't have to deal with the problems and stresses of ordinary life. Thus, it also carries the idea of being "carefree" or "without anxiety, dread, or fear."

Within the context of our verse, we can see that the doer is in a position to be envied by the hearer because God will bless or enlarge their doing of the Word. The doer can go through life without fear or anxiety because they are walking on the path of obedience, and their future is in the capable hands of Almighty God.

Putting It All Together

I hope these keyword studies have been as helpful to you as they have been to me. Combined with the context we gleaned in Chapters 6–8, these definitions have given us the information we need to interpret the Word faithfully. In the next chapter, we'll connect the dots using all the data we've gathered up to this point, and when we do, the whole picture will come into focus.

In the meantime, take a moment to jot down some of your own thoughts based on our keyword study. Which words struck you most powerfully? Which word pictures most helped you visualize what James is teaching us? Which parts of our passage have become clear to you, and where do you still have questions that need answered? Did any of the words add to your confusion? After you've made some notes to ponder as we interpret the Word together, I'll meet you in the next chapter.

_____

_____

_____

_____

_____

_____

_____

_____

_____

_____

_____

_____

CHAPTER 12

INTERPRET THE WORD

Be diligent to present yourself approved to God as a workman who does not need to be ashamed, accurately handling the word of truth.

—2 Tim. 2:15

If we have analyzed well, the previous chapters have given us the information we need to interpret the Word faithfully. However, I must be clear. This is the most dangerous of the eight steps to effective Bible study. We must not hastily rush to interpret the Word, for the Christian who interprets carelessly may be better off not studying Scripture at all. Many Christians have done untold damage to their faith and the faith of others through sloppy interpretation that results in false teaching disguised as spiritual-sounding doctrine.

In fact, several Christianity-based cults began in this very way. Poor interpretation sparked a thought that sounded good at the time but ultimately led to doctrine that now pushes people farther from Christ in the name of religion. That is why we must be thorough when we analyze and careful when we interpret. Those who analyze the Word poorly will interpret it incompletely at best and incorrectly at worst.

May we approach this step with humility, asking God to open our eyes to what we have not yet seen and make clear what we have not yet understood. Take a few moments to pray for God's grace and favor before we learn how to interpret the Word.

Begin with What Is Clear to You

It is not uncommon to get to this stage of Bible study and still have major questions that remain unanswered. While it can be tempting to obsess over these questions, I find it most helpful to begin with what is clear rather than what is not clear. Then, as you take time to prayerfully ponder the things you do understand, many of your questions will naturally answer themselves. Let me encourage you to pause here to make a list of the things you do understand. You might be surprised by how many of the puzzle pieces you already have in place.

For example, in our passage there are five big ideas that are very clear to me. First, *hearing the Word is important.* James is not criticizing the Christian who hears the Word; he is criticizing the Christian who *only* hears the Word and then fails to do what it says. James isn't against hearing the Word. He's simply saying that we can't stop there.

Second, *to hear the Word well, we must deal with our sin.* The abundance of sin within us functions like a buildup of earwax, keeping us from hearing well. Sin has a way of making Bible study seem dull and uninteresting. When we're harboring unrepentant sin, it will not be long before our desire for the Word wanes, and we don't want to receive the Word at all, let alone with a teachable spirit.

Third, *just as a mirror reflects my face, the Word of God reflects my heart.* The Bible is a spiritual mirror designed by God to show us what our hearts look like, and God's mirror never lies. Through His Word, God is faithful to show us where our hearts are not yet fully His, and in those areas, He calls us to make changes to our lives by the power of His indwelling Spirit.

Fourth, *the Bible isn't merely meant to be learned; it's meant to be lived.* This is massive, my friend. We are not here to understand the life-changing truths of Scripture; we are here to actually have our lives changed by Scripture. Let us press beyond merely hearing and walk in the joy and freedom of obedience.

Fifth, *there are several key differences between the hearer and the doer; these function as a sort of litmus test by which we evaluate ourselves.* For example, the doer and the hearer investigate the Word differently because they value it differently. In addition, the doer abides in the mirror long enough to put it into practice, while the hearer walks away and immediately forgets what they were going to change. Finally, while the hearer has made a grave spiritual miscalculation by failing to obey, the doer of the Word is blessed by God in what they do.

Now that I've defined what is clear, I know that anything that remains unclear to me must also fit within this framework. I'm sure you could add several additional thoughts and insights as well, so before we move on, let me encourage you to make your own list of what is clear to you. Don't fret over the things you don't yet understand. We'll get to those items in the next section.

Press On to Ponder What Is Not Yet Clear

Now that we've clarified what we do know, we can step back and reevaluate our questions in light of a partially completed puzzle. As we do, we pray that our questions will answer themselves as the Spirit opens our eyes to see and understand the truth.

For example, at this point, there were two things that were not yet clear to me. First, *I didn't understand why James used the word for a* male *to describe how the hearer looks in the mirror rather than the more common word for* mankind. Why is James picking on us, fellas?

And second, *we know that the hearer has miscalculated, but what has he miscalculated about?* Is this a minor miscalculation or a major *Honey I Shrunk the Kids* kind of miscalculation? What does the hearer forfeit when they fail to put the Word into practice?

I'm sure that if you pause for a moment to read and reconsider our passage, you'll have a few additional questions of your own. Take a few moments to make your own list, and prayerfully ponder how to make sense of each one in light of what you already know. Think through the historical and literary context. Is there anything that might clear up your confusion? And how might the keywords help answer your questions? As you ponder, pray that the Spirit will guide your thoughts and give you understanding.

Take your time and strive to form a full interpretation of our passage. In your own words, what is James saying, and why does it matter? Write your thoughts in the space provided on the following pages. Once you've interpreted the Word, I'll see you in the next section with a clear interpretation of James 1:21–25.

Your Interpretation of James 1:21–25

_____

_____

_____

_____

_____

_____

_____

_____

_____

_____

_____

_____

_____

_____

_____

_____

_____

_____

_____

INTERPRETATION OF JAMES 1:21–25

We know that James is writing from Jerusalem where he is the pastor of the Jerusalem church. His church people are suffering under an intense persecution at the hands of Saul (Acts 8:1), and many of them have fled for their lives to Judea and Samaria where James cannot physically pastor them. Thus, he is picking up his pen to write them a letter of encouragement, urging them to live on mission in Judea and Samaria despite the trials and temptations they will face in a new land (James 1:2–15).

In our particular passage, it is helpful to realize that while James' church members could not take their pastor to Judea and Samaria, they could take their Bibles. So, in our passage, James is urging his flock to receive and respond to the Word well because he knows they will need it desperately as they begin their new lives.

With that in mind, James tells his people in verse 21 to "put aside" or lay down once and for all the abundance of wickedness that remains in them. As we saw earlier, the sin within us functions like a buildup of earwax, keeping us from hearing the Word well. Yet James longs for his scattered flock to receive the Word with a teachable spirit, so he urges them to clean out their ears and lay down their sins once and for all. He reminds them that the Word is implanted in the soil of their hearts, which would remind them of Christ's parable of the Sower and the seed (Mark 4:1–20).

But simply hearing the Word is not enough. Next, James urges his flock to "prove themselves doers of the Word." A doer is an actor or entertainer, one who performs a script under the guidance of a director. In the same way, James views the Word as our script for how to live the Christian life. We are not called to merely learn and memorize our lines; we are called to act out what we see in the Word under the guidance of our director, the Holy Spirit.

In order for us to understand the difference between the hearer and the doer, James gives us an analogy to help us visualize how these two individuals interact with the Word. He pictures the Word as a mirror, which shows us the state of our hearts, and he describes the hearer as a male who looks in the mirror and walks away, immediately forgetting what he saw.

Now it's all making sense that James would pick on the men. Just as men and women generally tend to look in the mirror differently, hearers and doers also look into the Word differently. The hearer looks at the Word the same way men typically look in the mirror. They may look into the Word well enough to see clearly, but it's still more of a glance than a gaze. And hearers, like many men, often make the mistake of moving on too quickly, forgetting to take care of what the mirror revealed to be wrong.

But the doer "abides." They linger in the perfect law of liberty, almost like a woman getting ready for a romantic dinner. That is a deep, thorough self-examination we are talking about. Everything must be perfectly in place. And if anything is out of place, it is fixed before leaving the mirror. That is how the doer interacts with the Word, and that is why they are blessed in their doing.

This also explains what the hearer miscalculates. After all, the hearer assumes that they are also blessed. They assume that their hearing is "good enough," just like the man thinks his appearance is "good enough" after a glance in the mirror. However, James is clear that this is not the case. Blessing is reserved for the doer of the Word alone.

In other words, God is not ultimately impressed by how many sermons or podcasts you've listened to, books you've read, or verses you've memorized. To be clear, each of those things can be spiritually beneficial but only as they contribute to our becoming like Christ. The Christian who hears often and nonetheless fails to become more like Jesus isn't holy; according to James, they're a hypocrite.

So, this passage is almost like a three-step process to doing the Word. James says that if you're not hearing the Word well, then it's clear that you've got sin to lay down (step 1) so you can hear the Word with a humble and teachable spirit (step 2). But that's not all. The one who hears the Word well must press on to do the Word faithfully, applying the Scriptures to daily life by acting out what it says (step 3).

And speaking of the Word, James says the Scriptures are "able to save your souls" and refers to it as the "perfect law of liberty." These two phrases are absolutely significant. The Scriptures are God's primary means by which He delivers lost sinners from the penalty of eternal damnation, which means that God's law is not a law of bondage; it's the path out of bondage and into the joy and freedom of obedience.

With these truths in mind, how could we possibly settle for merely hearing the Word? My friend, know this. Untold blessings await the Christian who receives the Scriptures with humility and lives what they've learned. Let us be continually laying down sin, humbly welcoming the Word into our hearts, intently looking in the mirror, diligently abiding, and effectually doing according to all that is written in the Scriptures for us to do. May no sacrifice be too great and no obedience too much for us to give God our surrender. Let us be Christians who see the inestimable value of the Word and who learn to take God at His Word in our daily lives.

The Word doesn't specifically tell us that James' hearers listened to his words, but we do know that the gospel advanced rapidly throughout Judea and Samaria because "those who had been scattered went about preaching the word" (Acts 8:4). In other words, the persecution Saul brought upon the Jerusalem church led to the spread of the gospel in other regions. As the scattered believers proved themselves to be doers of the Word, they found opportunities to also be sharers of the Word, which led to the conversion of many souls (Acts 8:4–25; 9:31; 11:19–26).

Truly, our choice to be either a hearer or a doer of the Word will have a profound impact on the lives of others, just like these brothers and sisters who went before us. Like them, may we be effectual doers of the Word even in the darkest and most difficult seasons of our lives, and may God bless our doing to our own good and to the conversion of many souls. Amen.

Doers May Proceed

If you think about it, the hearer of James' analogy would be content to stop here. After all, we've looked in the mirror and understood our passage. We've learned what it means, and we can say that we've studied James 1:21–25. The only thing that remains is to prove ourselves doers, and that's the purpose of the rest of this book. You can walk away from this book now, but I believe doing so would be a great miscalculation. I believe God has great blessings in store for us as we continue on our journey to the life of a doer. I'm tenaciously pressing onward, and I invite you to join me.

FIRST INTERLUDE

MY PRAYER FOR YOU

For this reason I too, having heard of the faith in the Lord Jesus which exists among you and your love for all the saints, do not cease giving thanks for you, while making mention of you in my prayers; that the God of our Lord Jesus Christ, the Father of glory, may give to you a spirit of wisdom and of revelation in the knowledge of Him.

—Eph. 1:15–17

FATHER, THANK YOU for Your Word. It is beautiful, sacred, and practical. It is also clear that You never make me guess how I should live. I thank You for James 1:21–25. It's a passage that means so much to me. In a sense, I wish I could study this passage for the rest of my life, but I know there are many other powerful truths in Your Word, and I want to know them too. So, before I move on, I want to pray James 1:21–25 over myself, my family, my church, my community, our leaders, and all who will journey with me through this book.

Verse 21

God, You know that we are prone to allow filthiness and wickedness in our hearts, and You alone know how severe the cost of our sin has been. You know the pain, heartache, and guilt we have brought upon ourselves. You know the consequences we are facing for past actions. You know the prayers that have gone unanswered and the blessings that have been withheld by Your wise and righteous hand so we would see our need for repentance. You know how many times our sins have kept us from connecting with You and understanding Your Word.

So, Father, please help us. Give us grace to set aside all the filthiness that is hindering our fellowship with You. May we hold nothing back from You, O God. May there be nothing in our lives that we value so highly that we consider it to be worth sinning for. May we set aside our filthiness once and for all with no intention of ever picking it up again. We come to confess our sins. We long for a pure heart that is cleansed from all unrighteousness.

God, purify our hearts, and implant more of Your Word in us. Your Word is powerful. It is mighty to save. It is the gospel of God unto salvation. You have exalted it as high as Your Name. You have spoken to us in Your one and only Son, and You have authored it by Your Holy Spirit who indwells all those who trust in You. As I dwell on these realities for only a moment, Father, how could we receive Your Word with anything but humility? Give us a higher view of Your Word. Cause us to see it as You see it and value it as You value it. Give us the humility of Christ as we read, study, interpret, apply, and teach it to others.

Verse 22

Father, we aren't meant to merely study the Word; we are meant to live it. But when I consider our passage, the bar seems so high. You have called us to the life of a doer, but how incredible are the things You've called us to do! To be honest, being a doer seems impossible at times. Battling our flesh is often so discouraging. Many of us are living in defeat rather than victory and in despair rather than faith. It leaves us wondering if hearing the Word is the best we'll ever do. God, restore our hope that a life of victory and obedience is not beyond our reach.

Truly this is a lifestyle that is beyond our power. We cannot live godly lives without You, O God. Give us Your wisdom, grace, and strength as we study and apply the Bible to our lives. I know that if You have called us to the life of the doer, You will provide all that we need. May we trust You as we make the Word our lifestyle.

Verses 23–24

Father, it is clear that we must become passionately discontent with merely hearing the Word. May the analogy James gives us in these verses shake us at the core of our beings. How quick we are to look in the mirror and correct flaws in our physical appearance, and yet those are only flaws with our earthly bodies.

When weighed against our souls, how little does it matter to have hairs out of place, shaving cream behind the ears, or a smudge of lipstick on our teeth?

But if we care so thoroughly for our physical appearances, how much more thoroughly should we examine and care for our souls. Lord, please forgive us for our carelessness, and open our eyes to see how valuable our souls are. Teach us to prize our souls as highly as Your Son, who gave His life to redeem them.

Verse 25

Please, Father, help us study Your Word as this verse describes. May we "look intently" into the mirror of Your perfect law. May we come to Your Word hungry for more of You. You are our treasure, our prize, and our greatest joy. We long to know You more. We long to walk in Your ways. We long to bring You glory.

Lord, may we all become effectual doers of Your Word who reap the blessings and joys of living in obedience to You. Thank You for communicating Your truth and Yourself to us in the Scriptures. Teach us to rightly value Your Word. We praise the Father for loving us enough to give His Son for us. We praise the Son for being our perfect example of righteousness. We praise the Spirit for guiding us into all truth and empowering us to live as Jesus lived.

Father, I pray specifically for each person who reads this book. Thank You for them. You love each of them with a love they'll never comprehend. Give them a deep hunger for Your Word. Grant them a passion that persists through the difficult and tedious days of study. May Your Spirit open their eyes to understand truth as they study, and may they delight in You as they learn of Your works and Your ways. Ultimately, may we all fall more in love with You than ever before. Amen.

PART 2

HOW TO MEDITATE ON THE WORD

CHAPTER 13

MEDITATE ON THE WORD – PART 1

O how I love Your law!
It is my meditation all the day.

—Ps. 119:97

WHEN WAS THE last time you took a few minutes to simply consider the beauty and majesty of God? We certainly don't pause often enough, but I believe it would benefit our spiritual lives tremendously if we would stop periodically to take our focus off of ourselves, our agendas, and our problems and dwell on the wonder, perfection, and glory of Almighty God.

Look up at the night sky, and then consider that God set all the heavenly bodies in their proper places (Job 38:31–33). Think of the matchless beauty and wisdom of the world He created for us to dwell in (Gen. 1–2). Ponder the multitude of blessings and joys that He freely showers upon us (Eph. 1:3) and think of the depths of His love toward us in Christ (Eph. 3:14–21).

Consider the fallen angels who sinned against God only one time and yet are without the hope of salvation (Heb. 2:16), while we who sin against God over and over again are freely offered salvation by grace through Christ Jesus (Eph. 2:1–10). Think of the millions of prayers that are being offered up to God in various languages and dialects at this very moment, yet if we were to start praying as well, He would hear and respond to every word we say (1 John 5:15).

Consider the matchless love of God who poured out His wrath on His innocent Son for us. Consider also the matchless love of Jesus who left behind the unimaginable joys of heaven to become a "man of sorrows and acquainted with grief" in accomplishing our salvation (Isa. 53:3). Consider that Christ had never before aroused the wrath of His Father, and yet He bore the wrath of God in full for you and me (Isa. 53:4–11).

None of this is new information. But sometimes it's helpful to pause and let what we already know *sink in*. That's the goal of our next step in the Bible study process—meditating on the Word. Before we can live the Word well, it must first sink into our hearts well. Because *meditation* is a word loaded with meaning, much of which is based on faulty ideas, let's begin our discussion by taking a closer look at what biblical meditation is and how it will aid our growth in the Scriptures.

Biblical Meditation Is Mind-Oriented

One of the main Hebrew words for meditate in the Old Testament is *sîyach*, which literally means "to mumble or stutter." The word carries the idea of getting swept away in thought over something, seriously pondering a matter or thinking deeply about a subject.[11] Think of someone who is so absorbed in their thoughts that they talk to themselves, oblivious to their surroundings, and you've got the idea. To meditate on the Word is to get lost in thought over God and His truth. It is to get swept away in worshipful contemplation of God's character and His wonderful works.

This biblical understanding is consistent with how the meaning of the word evolved over time. The word *meditate* is derived from the root word *med*, which refers to taking "appropriate measures" to do something correctly. Over time, the word began to carry the idea of "contemplation, devout preoccupation, private devotions, and prayer." In Old French, the word *meditacion* referred to "thought, reflection, and study," and the Old Latin *meditationem* meant "to think over, reflect, or consider." Later, the Latin verb usage carried even stronger connotations such as "to plan, devise, practice, rehearse, and study."[11] We can see from all these definitions that meditation is something rational, something cognitive. Meditation is not a feeling or an emotion; it is an intentional act of the mind. In fact, that's our next point.

Biblical Meditation Is Intentional

To meditate is to set your mind on something, to focus your thoughts on a particular idea or goal that deserves the time you can devote to it. Meditation implies serious contemplation and study, not allowing your mind to wander or emptying your mind altogether. Biblically speaking, meditation refers to deliberately focusing our minds on the wonderful character of God and on His Word while we diligently fight against the distractions that would keep us from knowing and loving Him more.[12] See how this understanding of meditation helps us understand Paul's words to the church at Philippi:

> *Finally, brethren, whatever is true, whatever is honorable, whatever is right, whatever is pure, whatever is lovely, whatever is of good repute, if there is any excellence and if anything worthy of praise, **dwell on these things*** (bold emphasis added).
>
> —Phil. 4:8

Amen. There's no such thing as a useful believer with a lazy mind. Maturity in the faith cannot come apart from biblical meditation.

Taking in truth through Bible study or listening to sermons and podcasts is certainly important, but have you noticed how often we can take in truth without it really sinking in? Just as we must chew and swallow our food in order to derive benefit from it, so we must also "chew on" the truths of Scripture as God reveals them to us. God gave us minds to dwell on His majesty and glory, but godly thinking doesn't just happen; it's an intentional choice we make daily as we seek to love and worship Him with all our minds (Matt. 22:36–37).

Biblical Meditation Is Worship

The word *meditate* is found 22 times in the New American Standard Bible 1995 translation, and 18 of those times are in the book of Psalms, the hymnal of the Bible.[13] That teaches us that *meditation is an act of worship*. And that makes sense. After all, to meditate on something is to devote significant amounts of thought and energy to it, which means we meditate only on the things we deem worthy of all that time and mental energy. Whatever we consistently meditate on is what we deem to be most important. It's the object of our worship.

My friend, God is not only worthy of your singing; *He is worthy of your thinking*. His Word is worthy of your worshipful contemplation. His majesty is worthy of your deep and humble reflection. His works and His ways are often mysterious, higher than our minds can comprehend and deeper than the deepest waters of the sea (Isa. 55:8–9). Are they not worthy of our striving to understand so we might worship Him for His marvelous works?

After all, what else could be more worthy of our meditation? Ourselves? Our money? Our careers? No, my friend! May we get swept away in thoughts of worshipful meditation focused on the King of heaven and earth. May we long for intimacy with our Father as the sailor longs for the sea. May we learn to delight in His truth and love Him with all our hearts, souls, minds, and strength (Matt. 22:36–37).

Biblical Meditation Is Relational

We have already seen that Bible study is a relational event and that meditating on the Scriptures is no less relational. As we meditate, we ask the Spirit to guide us "into all the truth" (John 16:13) by taking biblical truths that are still foggy to us and making them clear (Ps. 119:18). We pray that He will set our often cold and indifferent hearts on fire with the truths of Scripture. We seek His guidance as to how we should apply the truths we've learned, and we ask for the power only He can provide to live out what we've learned under His teaching (Gal. 5:16–26).

Don't miss how desperately we need the Holy Spirit in every aspect of Bible study. To meditate on the Word apart from the Spirit is to attempt to understand Scripture with our own finite and futile minds. We need God's Spirit in order to meditate fruitfully on His Word.

Of course, as we meditate, we also interact with the Father and Son. Our meditations on the Word will naturally lead to a heart of humble gratitude toward the Father. We praise His holy name, giving thanks to Him for communicating His truth to us. We exalt and glorify Jesus Christ without whom we would have no hope of eternal life. We commit to following Him and making disciples in His name. Meditation brings us into direct and worshipful interaction with each member of the Trinity. What could possibly be more important than this? God, help us see the importance of meditating on Your Word. We'll learn more about what this looks like in the next chapter.

CHAPTER 14

MEDITATE ON THE WORD – PART 2

I have more insight than all my teachers,
For Your testimonies are my meditation.

—Ps. 119:99

BY THIS POINT in our study, we've prepared for the Word and analyzed the context, key words, and any other helpful clues we could find. We've connected the dots as the Spirit has given us clarity. It seems as though we've gone as deep into James 1:21–25 as possible and gained all there is to know about what God is saying, but there is much more to learn.

The reality is that we understand our passage like a kid who can't swim understands the pool. We may have dipped our feet in the water and gotten wet—and that's important—but we haven't really learned to swim around in this passage until we've meditated on what it teaches. When we meditate on the Word, we're moving beyond the milk of the Word and beginning to chew the nourishing meat of truth (Heb. 5:11–14). That is where the Bible starts to really come alive in our hearts and minds. Before we consider a few practical tips for biblical meditation, let's consider some of the reasons Scripture encourages us to meditate.

To Foster Obedient Hearts

This book of the law shall not depart from your mouth, but you
shall meditate on it day and night, so that you may be careful to
do according to all that is written in it; for then you will make
your way prosperous, and then you will have success.

—Josh. 1:8

Have you ever wondered why there's an ever-increasing gap between how much of the Bible we *know* and how much of the Bible we *live*? Why is it that we can hear a sermon or study a passage and rejoice in the truths we've learned and yet somehow fail to live in them? Why are so many of us struggling to be doers of the Word and not merely hearers who delude themselves?

Joshua 1:8 is commonly quoted in Christian circles. We use it to encourage one another to devote more and more time to the serious reading and study of the Word, and rightly so. But have you noticed *why* God told Joshua to meditate on the book of the law day and night? It was so he would be careful to do all that is written in it.

You see, it wasn't enough for Joshua to simply study the book of the law. God had called him to do it—*all of it.* And in this verse, God gives Joshua the key to the life of the doer that many of us have either ignored or given up on. The key to Joshua's obedience—and the key to our obedience today—is meditating on Scripture.

Meditation is the bridge that runs between our heads and our hearts, allowing God's truth to transform both our thinking and our living. Meditation is designed by God to take biblical truths that we've learned and make them a conscious reality that we live in for the glory of God. A life of consistent obedience simply cannot happen apart from meditation on the Word. In fact, I would go so far as to say that if I understand the Word but don't apply it, that means I'm not spending enough time meditating on the Word.

That is where we can most clearly see what we've forfeited by neglecting biblical meditation. We have become people with full heads and empty hearts. When did we buy into the lie that Bible study was more about understanding God than becoming like God? When did we forget that the truths of the Word are real, that what we're studying matters eternally and is meant to be lived?

When we meditate on the Word, we're reminded that these are truths that if implanted in our hearts will deeply impact who we are and how we live. These are realities that will radically transform our relationships, the way we approach our work, and the delight we experience in God. Once biblical principles move from our heads to our hearts, we simply have to do the things that we're seeing in the Word. They have become part of who we *are*, not just part of what we *know*.

To Keep from Worry and Fear

Even though princes sit and *talk against me,*
Your servant meditates on Your statutes.

—Ps. 119:23

This is one of those verses that I need to meditate on much more. David is being plotted against by princes—people with the power and authority to do him great harm or even bring him to death (consider King Saul's murderous intentions as one possible example). An attack could come from anywhere at any moment. He's not safe.

I don't know how you would handle this situation, but if I were David, I would be diligently watching my back or working to ensure my own safety. I would try to learn of my enemies' plans against me so I could avoid walking into a trap. I would perhaps go on the offensive and try to do them harm before they can get to me. I would sleep with one eye open at night. I wouldn't allow myself to move freely or trust anyone. I would let their designs against me consume my thoughts.

In other words, I would *meditate* on their plans against me. And we do this all the time. *Worrying is simply meditating on the things we're afraid of.*

But David takes a radically different approach that at first seems remarkably stupid. His life is in danger, and his response to his situation is to meditate on the statutes in God's Word. Is he really going to act like his life isn't in danger? Isn't that the same as burying his head in the sand?

By God's grace, I've come to see the wisdom of David's ways and why this verse is included in the Scriptures "for our instruction" (Rom. 15:4). I believe David is meditating on the Word so he knows how to conduct himself, even when his life is on the line. Looming danger has a way of playing on our minds, filling our heads with all sorts of fears and paranoia, and I'm sure it could easily have been so with David. Instead, he chose to ground his mind by meditating on the truths of Scripture. That gave him the perspective he needed to navigate his circumstances well.

David had learned that the solutions to our problems can't be discovered by excessively fixating on the problems themselves. Can worrying about your credit card debt teach you how to climb out of the hole? Can dwelling on your struggles with sexual sin equip you to live in purity? Can obsessing over a fight with your spouse or a friend supply you with the perspective you need to be a peacemaker?

No, my friend! We must go to the Word with our problems and seek wisdom by meditating on God's statutes. Psalm 1 indicates that the one who meditates on the Word "will be like a tree *firmly* planted by streams of water, which yields its fruit in its season and its leaf does not wither; and in whatever he does, he prospers" (Ps. 1:3). That's the kind of life I long to live. Even in life's most difficult and trying times, we can meditate on the Word and find that it is a lamp for our feet (Ps. 119:105).

To Remember the Works of God

> *I will meditate on all Your work*
> *And muse on Your deeds.*
>
> —Ps. 77:12

> *Make me understand the way of Your precepts,*
> *So I will meditate on Your wonders.*
>
> —Ps. 119:27

In addition to meditating on the Word, we can derive great benefit from meditating on the works of God. We are a forgetful people, prone to rejoicing in God's works one day only to doubt His kindness the next. But meditating on the works of God is one way to remind ourselves of His power, majesty, and goodness. That is why the children of Israel so frequently set up memorials; they served as a visual reminder of God's great and powerful works (Gen. 28:10–22; 35:9–15; Exod. 24:1–8; Deut. 27:1–8; Josh. 4:19–24; 1 Sam. 7:7–14).

These memorials were meant to serve as a reminder of God's faithfulness to future generations of Israel. Because of these visual tributes to God's majesty, His people could not only look back on the past with deep thankfulness but could also look to the future with great confidence in God.

With these realities in mind, last year I began keeping a journal that I call my Answered Prayer Journal. Every week, I write down praises, answered prayers, and other examples of God's power and glory that I've either seen or heard about.

It's difficult to put into words how often I have received refreshment at this well. When my soul has felt dry, reading my Answered Prayer Journal has been a source of great refreshment for me. When my faith has felt weak, the journal has helped my unbelief and caused me to hope in God again. When my heart has felt faint, it has given me renewed courage to live passionately for King Jesus.

TIPS FOR MEDITATING ON THE WORD

Remove Anything That Hinders Your Focus

Now that we've come to an understanding of what biblical meditation is and why it's important, let's examine some practical advice that might help you make this a regular spiritual discipline. A few of the tips I could share in this chapter are already in Chapter 4, Prepare for the Word. For the sake of brevity, I won't repeat those tips here, but I would encourage you to go back and review them, this time considering how you could best utilize them during your time in meditation. The rest of this section will deal with additional advice that relates specifically to meditating on the Word.

Determine When You Will Meditate

There's an old Scottish proverb that says, "What may be done at any time will be done at no time." What gets scheduled typically gets done, and what doesn't get scheduled typically is forgotten. If we are going to succeed in making biblical meditation a consistent spiritual discipline, we must determine when and how we will meditate on the Word. There are two primary approaches that I have seen work well.

First, some people set aside a devoted chunk of time each day to meditate on the Scriptures they're studying. One of my closest friends uses a specific chair in his office and devotes each lunch period to Scripture meditation and prayer. Several others meditate on the Word in the evenings before bed. Personally, I have incorporated meditation into my morning time with God. I'm simply not finished spending time with God until I have spent a good chunk of time in meditation on the Word.

However, I also know some people who meditate throughout the day as they have the opportunity to do so. It's a meditate-without-ceasing approach, if you will. So, when they're standing in line, sitting in traffic, or enjoying a brief respite of down time, they refuse to get on their phones and instead choose to meditate on the Word. I have tried this method and found that it doesn't work for me as well as devoting a chunk of time to meditation, but perhaps this method will work for you. Either way, the idea here is that meditation is a spiritual discipline, and it won't happen by accident. Find a time or place that works best for you, and in time you will reap tremendous spiritual benefits from your time in meditation.

Meditate Specifically

Meditating specifically is perhaps the most important thing I've experienced that might help your time in meditation. When I first began the practice of meditating on the Word, I took a passage such as James 1:21–25 and attempted to meditate on it all at once. That quickly became overwhelming because there were so many important truths to dwell on.

So let me encourage you to get specific. Don't try to dwell on multiple truths all at once. Meditate on one at a time. Each truth is a springboard from which God can direct your thoughts. Perhaps you'd like to meditate on what it looks like to "put aside all filthiness and all that remains of wickedness." From there, you might consider what it means to "abide" in the perfect law of liberty. Wherever you start, let me encourage you to get specific and focus on one truth at a time.

Meditate Prayerfully

As you focus on a particular phrase or biblical truth, approach it prayerfully, asking questions of God and of your own heart as you go. Now I must warn you that *the answers you seek won't always come easily, and you will be tempted to quit.* We are now navigating the deep and turbulent waters of the heart where progress and understanding come slowly and only to those who are willing to persevere with God. It is as we meditate on the Word that the Father reveals to us our deepest fears, reminds us of the hurts that have cut most deeply, and exposes the lies of the enemy that we have believed and agreed with to our own detriment. These realities are difficult for us to accept and tough to come to terms with.

Even now, perhaps you can sense something within you welling up in resistance to the idea of facing these realities in your own heart. There are parts of our hearts that we long to keep hidden, and the thought of God drawing them out into the open and exposing them to the light can be terrifying.

But don't miss the beauty in this. God is a tender Father who draws out the hidden areas of our hearts, not to leave us in shame and despair but to provide the hope and healing that our souls deeply need. Like a skilled physician, He reveals to us those things that are keeping us from a spiritually healthy and abundant life and treats them with the gentle salve of the Word.

As you enter into prayerful meditation on the Word, remember that God longs to make more of His heart known to you, so humble yourself before Him. Ask Him to connect the dots for you. Delight in Him, and desire His glory above everything else. Be sensitive to each gentle nudge the Spirit uses to direct your heart. Commit to obedience in advance. Surrender yourself wholeheartedly to do His will. Trust that He has your best in mind and wants to lead you into deeper communion with Christ. Give Him thanks as His majesty becomes clearer to you.

SECOND INTERLUDE

A TEMPLATE FOR PERSONAL MEDITATION

I will meditate on Your precepts and regard Your ways.

—Ps. 119:15

BEFORE WE MOVE on to applying the Word, I want to share an example of my own meditations. This past week, I took a break from my studies in Jude to meditate specifically on James 1:22. I don't usually journal my meditations on Scripture, but this time I made an exception so I could sincerely meditate on our passage and also have thoughts to refer to later and share with you. If you're new to meditating on Scripture, you can use this as a template to help you get started. My prayer is that the meditations and prayers of my heart in the pages ahead will provide an example for your own meditations on the Word.

Meditations on James 1:22

God, there is clearly a difference between the hearer and the doer. What does this look like practically? Spell this out for me, and help me understand what You are saying. I don't think I'm seeing everything. It's not as clear to me as it could be. Open my eyes, Father. Connect the dots for me. I want to be a doer of Your Word. I want to be like my Jesus.

After a few minutes of prayerful consideration, I found my thoughts being directed back to our passage. I remembered that James doesn't use the same Greek word for *look* with regard to the hearer and the doer. As I continued to think this through, the contrasts between the hearer and the doer began to make more sense to me.

Clearly, the doer is looking for the purpose of *change*. The doer is not moving on from the mirror of the Word without fixing whatever needs to be changed. But the hearer is content to have only *seen* and *understood* what they looked like.

Ouch! I do that more than I'd like to admit. Okay, God. Thanks for showing me this. The passage makes much more sense now. So, when I spend time in Your Word, which one am I like?

I must pause here to share with you that the most dangerous part of meditating on the Word comes right after we ask God a heart question. If we want a certain answer, we can try to manufacture that answer in our minds and then attribute it to God. But it is important to be sincere and seek all the answers we *need* to hear, not the ones we *want* to hear.

It took me a few minutes to wrestle through this desire for a pleasing answer. Deep down, I want to be a doer of the Word, so I had to settle in my own heart that the truth was more important than an answer that puffs up my pride. I stopped to sincerely ask God to show me my heart as it really is, not as I wish it were. Before long, God started unpacking my heart and the filthiness that still lies within me.

The reality that hit me is that I am a doer of the Word—*when it's easy or convenient.* I don't mind being a doer of the Word 95 percent of the time, but there are times when I see clearly in the mirror and choose not to fix what I see because it would require too much effort or cause me to give up something I love more than I should. In these moments, I've heard the Word. I've seen myself clearly, but I would rather *forget* than *do.* In fact, now that I think of it, maybe the hearer doesn't always intend to be a hearer. Maybe they start out hoping to be a doer, but they settle for hearing because it's easier to forget the sinfulness of the heart than repent and change.

Yes, that's it. They settle. Like a man before a mirror, *the hearer is more easily satisfied with their appearance than a doer.* After all, a woman is not typically content to leave the mirror until her appearance is exactly as she thinks it should be. There is seldom "good enough" for a woman looking in the mirror. The same is true for the doer as they stand before the mirror of the Word. But the hearer doesn't want to put in all that effort. It seems obsessive to them. So hearers lie to themselves. They delude themselves into thinking that if they look "good enough" for themselves, God must be pleased too.

Yikes! I do that too. I'm far too easily satisfied with my spiritual life, and I assume that God is as satisfied with my spiritual life as I am.

Now I must be clear. This wasn't fun in the moment. Meditating on the Word often places us on the receiving end of God's loving and gentle conviction, and we can be pretty sensitive. In those moments, I tend to get mad. I get defensive and try to make excuses. I want to quit meditating. I want to walk away from the mirror.

But God brings those thoughts to mind for a reason. He isn't picking a fight; He is introducing us to the joy of surrender. He is showing us our spiritual MRI results so we can see our desperate need for the Great Physician.

Yes, conviction hurts—sometimes very deeply. Many of the most soul-wrenching moments of my life have happened while meditating on the Word. But why should I expect anything else? Did I really think it would be a painless process for God to make me more like His Son?

Remember this, my friend. When God fires up the furnace, it's to *refine* you, not to *burn* you. You may initially want to resist the pain of God's loving conviction, but learn to embrace it as His grace and favor toward you. On the other side of the pain of conviction He provides the healing, comfort, and joy your soul deeply longs for. Receive conviction with thankfulness and let God's kindness lead you to repentance (Rom. 2:4).

Well, after arguing with God for longer than I'd like to admit, God finally broke me down. For the next 20 minutes or so, God was gracious to show me several specific areas of my life where I had settled for being a hearer of the Word. That was hard to receive, but it was so freeing.

Alright, God, I see it now, and I agree with You. I'm not wholly surrendered. I'm holding part of my life and part of myself back from You. I am too easily satisfied with my spiritual life. I'm trying to live for you 95 percent of the time, but I reserve 5 percent of my life for myself. God, help me see the foolishness of this. I'm willing to change. I know Jesus died to redeem and save all of me and that I am not my own. I acknowledge that You alone are worthy of all my heart. I don't want to hold anything back from You. I want to be a doer in every area of life. Show me what that looks like. Give me Your grace and Your favor. Strengthen me because I am weak.

At this point it seemed wise to begin prayerfully thinking through how to apply what I'd learned by meditating on our passage. I asked God to give me direction and guide my thoughts toward the actions and habits that He has in mind for me.

Over the next few minutes, my thoughts landed on a few ways to apply these verses to my life. Before I share them with you in the next chapter, let me encourage you to put this book down for at least three days to practice prayerful meditation on the truths we've learned together in James 1:21–25.

Spend some time on each phrase of our passage. Ask God sincere questions and be willing for Him to reveal and heal the things in your heart that you have longed to keep hidden. Let the One who implanted the Word in your head use it as a salve for your heart. Repent fully and specifically when you're convicted of sin. Surrender yourself wholeheartedly to do His will and ask Him to make the truths of James 1:21–25 a living reality in your life. Thank God for His grace and mercy toward you, and that He cares so deeply for your heart that He sent His Son to die for you and His Spirit to minister to you through the Word. Take as much time as you need, and when you're ready I'll see you in the next chapter.

PART 3

HOW TO DO THE WORD

CHAPTER 15

APPLY THE WORD

Therefore everyone who hears these words of Mine and acts on them, may be compared to a wise man who built his house on the rock.

—Matt. 7:24

BY GOD'S GRACE and through diligent study, we now know what the Spirit is trying to communicate to us through James 1:21–25. But the end goal of Bible study is not understanding; it is action. Knowledge of the Scriptures is important, but its main purpose is to transform our thoughts, behaviors, and actions. According to our passage, if we hear the Word and yet fail to apply it, our study time has ultimately been a waste.

We've already seen what it means to be a doer of the Word. The doer is an actor, someone who performs under the direction and guidance of another. The Christian is one who lives out their faith under the direction of the Spirit, following the example of Jesus Christ according to the will of God the Father. The Christian life isn't for those who want to sit on the sidelines and take in a show. *As followers of Jesus, our lives are the show.* As we live from a renewed heart, we point everyone around us to the majesty of Jesus our King (Matt. 5:13–16). Let's look at a few practical suggestions that will serve you well as you seek to apply the Word to your life.

Be Specific

When it comes to applying the Word, one of the most common mistakes I see Christians make is being vague. Resist the temptation to settle for lazy, generic applications, and resolve to be specific and clear about how you will live out the truth. Take time to determine specifically how you will obey God's Word by His grace, and you will be more likely to follow through on obedient living.

For example, an ambiguous application of our passage would be this: "I need to stop being a hearer of the Word and start being a doer." While this might be true, there is nothing specific to follow through on. Instead, consider precisely what you will do. Perhaps you need to list three specific applications for every Bible passage you study and commit to implement them within the next 48 hours. Maybe you'll want to find someone who can hold you accountable to applying the Word. It might even be helpful to implement some sort of reward system for every time you follow through on doing the Word (ice cream and cinnamon rolls, anyone?).

Remember, friends, the enemy has no issue with you understanding the Word—as long as you don't live it. The Christian who merely hears the Word is not a threat to the forces of darkness, but the doer of the Word will face fierce opposition. The enemy longs to waste all the time and effort you've invested in the Word by convincing you to walk away as a hearer. So do not be surprised if you get to this stage of Bible study and suddenly feel apathetic about what you've learned or if life's circumstances make it very difficult for you to apply what you're studying. Spiritual warfare often hits us here because this is the crucial step of Bible study. All else depends on what we do with what we've learned.

Be Enthusiastic

Every time we study the Word, there should be a tension between wanting to continue our studies and wanting to put the Bible down so we can put into practice the new and exciting truths we're learning. If that tension doesn't exist, then we're either studying for the wrong reasons or we're failing to really grasp the power of what we're learning. For me, this is typically an indication that I need to meditate on the passage a bit more because it is during my time in meditation that God gives me a sense of delight in what I'm learning and an urgency to put it into practice.

The point here is that Scripture application shouldn't be a joyless chore. After all, Bible application is not about following the rules so you don't get punished; it's about imitating Christ and living in His freedom and joy. With each new step toward obedience, we're participating more fully in the abundant life that Christ delights for us to experience, so let's get excited about applying the Bible!

Be Wholistic

When we think of Scripture application, we most often picture a change in actions. But as we'll see, applying Scripture is far more than just behavior modification. God wants to use Scripture to transform *all of me*. Practically speaking, that means no topics are off limits as we study the Bible. Every area of our lives is subject to being placed under the microscope of Scripture, including the areas that make us uncomfortable. May we relentlessly wrestle with the truths of the Bible and how they guide us in godliness as we follow Jesus in this crazy, unpredictable world.

In fact, I believe this is the primary reason our Bible application is often ineffective. We seek to change our behavior without also submitting the rest of ourselves to the authority of Scripture. But this betrays our half-heartedness when it comes to applying the Bible. Can we really expect to perform godly actions while also refusing to submit our thoughts, beliefs, loves, attitudes, and words to the Word?

With that in mind, let's examine a wholistic approach to Bible application that places our whole lives under the authority of the Word. Wholistic application goes beyond behavior modification to the heart, mind, soul, and strength of a person.

A WHOLISTIC APPROACH

Beliefs — How Should This Reinforce My Faith?

> *Behold, as for the proud one, his soul is not right within him; but the righteous will live by his faith.*
>
> —Hab. 2:4

Fundamentally speaking, application is the test of whether or not we *really* believe God's Word. After all, our beliefs ultimately determine our behaviors, so if we aren't living out what we've studied, it can only be because we haven't taken God at His Word.

Instead of wondering how we should act differently, perhaps the first question we should ask ourselves is how we might believe differently. How should what we've just studied impact our faith in God? Some passages will prompt us to radically change our beliefs to align them with God's Word, and other passages will cement convictions that we already hold to. Either way, there is great benefit to be derived from sincerely meditating on this.

God has used our passage to reinforce my belief that God's commands are for our good and that obedience is meant to be a delight, not a chore. God's commands are not burdensome; they are the way to life and peace. Abundant joy belongs to those who take God at His Word and choose to walk in His ways (Ps. 119:1–2).

Take a few moments to consider how our passage should change your beliefs, and write some of your thoughts here: _____

_____ _____

_____

Affection – How Should This Refresh My Worship?

> *God is spirit, and those who worship Him must worship in spirit and truth.*
>
> —John 4:24

If our Bible study hasn't resulted in praise, then the truth hasn't reached our hearts. Every truth of Scripture should cause us to fall more in love with Jesus. Every principle we learn ought to bring us to our knees in humble adoration and willing service. Every passage we study should deepen and refresh our worship.

How can our passage do this? I've been reminded of how difficult it is to live out the Word. My flesh longs for the pleasures of this world, and I often feel weak and powerless to obey, even when I want to. That reminder has given me a deeper appreciation for Jesus, the perfect Doer of the Word. He is my merciful and faithful High Priest who sympathizes with me in my deep weakness (Heb. 2:17). Through Him I may boldly approach the throne of grace for help as I seek to follow His example of joyful surrender (Heb. 4:14–16).

I'm so deeply thankful that my help comes through the Holy Spirit, my Helper (John 14:26). Apart from the Spirit, I would be powerless to obey the Scriptures. Think of it. What a terrible agony it would be to know God's truth and yet be powerless to walk in the freedom it offers us. If I pause for a few moments to consider what my life would look like apart from the Spirit of God, it thoroughly shakes my soul. How can I not worship the One who has saved me from such agony?

Take a few moments to consider how our passage should change your affections, and write some of your thoughts here: _____

_____

_____

Thoughts – How Should This Renew My Mind?

> *And do not be conformed to this world, but be transformed by the renewing of your mind, so that you may prove what the will of God is, that which is good and acceptable and perfect.*
>
> —Rom. 12:2

Every time we interact with Scripture, we're reminded that God's thoughts are far superior to our own (Isa. 55:8–9). Even though Christians "have the mind of Christ" (1 Cor. 2:16), our thought lives often reflect faulty beliefs and sinful tendencies that hinder our growth to spiritual maturity. Thus, when we come to the Word, we seek to have our minds renewed by the Word of truth (Rom. 12:1–2).

Truly, if we do not think like Christ, we will not live like Christ. So how should we think differently as a result of our passage in James? For me, I now have a different perspective on hearing the Word. I now think about hearing as Christ does. *Hearing* was never meant to be an end in itself; it was always meant to lead us into the deeper fruitfulness of *doing* the Word. I now think of hearing and not doing as a grave error. It is an offense to God who is worthy of my worshipful life of obedience. I now resolve never to stop short of obedience in Bible study.

Take a few moments to consider how our passage should change your thought patterns. Write some of your thoughts here: _____

_____

_____

Attitudes – How Should This Revise My Outlook?

> *Rejoice always; pray without ceasing; in everything give thanks; for this is God's will for you in Christ Jesus.*
> —1 Thess. 5:16–18

World-renowned leadership expert John Maxwell once remarked that we are either the masters or the victims of our attitudes.[16] What a powerful truth! Few things will determine the course of our lives as much as the attitudes we choose. Thus, we must let the Spirit cultivate godly attitudes in us through the Word.

I can't tell you how many times God has spared me from poor choices and devastating errors with a simple attitude adjustment. With regard to our passage, I have to admit that I am often discouraged because of my many sins. I feel weak and unworthy as if holiness will always be out of reach. But in James 1, the Word reminds me that God has designed for me to walk in obedience as a doer. Sin is no longer my master, and I can mortify the flesh by the power of the Spirit (Rom. 6:12–14; 8:12–17; Col. 3:5–10).

And this drastically changes my attitude. No longer do I want to give up and throw in the towel. No longer does the command to "be holy, for I am holy" (1 Pet. 1:16) seem to be impossible, out of reach, or something I should give up on. You and I can look at holiness with hope because I am "confident of this very thing, that He who began a good work in you will perfect it until the day of Christ Jesus" (Phil. 1:6).

We often underestimate the power of the Word to impart to us godly attitudes. As you study, let the Spirit direct your outlook until you see your circumstances and experiences from His perspective and not your own. Let God show you how to feel about your life, how to approach your trials, and how to evaluate your past. You'll be amazed at how often God gives you hope where the world only sows panic and despair.

Take a few moments to consider how our passage should change your attitudes, and write some of your thoughts here: _____

_____

_____

Priorities – How Should This Redeem My Time?

Therefore be careful how you walk, not as unwise men but as wise, making the most of your time, because the days are evil.
—Eph. 5:15–16

Have you ever wondered why animal trainers carry a stool when they go into a cage of lions? The trainers have their whips and pistols, of course, but they also carry a stool. William H. Hinson explains that this stool is actually "the most important tool of the trainer." When the wild animal starts to act out, the trainer holds the stool at the top and thrusts the legs toward the lion's face. In the lion's attempt to focus on all four legs at once, a kind of paralysis overwhelms it, and it becomes tame because its attention has become fragmented.[15]

That pretty accurately sums up the Christian life in a fallen world. Every day we are bombarded with distractions, urgent needs, and important matters. Our attempts to focus on everything can leave us feeling overwhelmed, spiritually dry, and on the brink of burnout. In a day where everything seems urgent and everyone wants to tell you what is most important, we must let God determine that and set our priorities through His Word.

As we spend time in the Word, we're reminded that life is about more than just going to work, paying bills, getting the kids through college, and hoping you have enough saved up for retirement. There are immense spiritual realities that we often forget about or neglect because the world has shoved a multitude of "stool legs" in our face. If we aren't careful to submit our priorities to God, we will live busy lives that leave little impact on the kingdom. Let us live for what God says is important, even if it costs us in this world.

Take a few moments to consider how our passage should change your priorities, and write some of your thoughts here: _____

_____

_____

Tongue – How Should This Refine My Words?

Let the words of my mouth and the meditation of my heart be acceptable in Your sight, O LORD, my rock and my Redeemer.

—Ps. 19:14

Research shows that the average person speaks at least 7,000 words per day.[16] With that in mind, we shouldn't be surprised if Scripture application will have as much of an impact on our words as it does on our actions. Indeed, a major part of our growth to spiritual maturity includes learning to master the tongue (James 1:26; 3:1–12).

This makes sense, right? It is difficult to accurately express the immense influence that words have had on human history. Words have deceived, and they have empowered. Words have given hope to the discouraged, and they have led multitudes astray. Words have been instrumental in building nations from the ground up, and they have brought whole empires to their knees. In fact, God Himself demonstrated the enormous power of the tongue by *speaking* His creation into existence (Ps. 33:6–9).

If the Christian life is about imitating Christ, then we must also imitate His speech. Only the Word can instruct us on how to speak words "with grace" and "seasoned with salt" (Col. 4:6). Only through the Spirit can we learn to harness "every careless word," avoid gossip, and speak "the truth in love" (Matt. 12:36; Prov. 20:19; Eph. 4:15).

Take a few moments to consider how our passage should change your speech, and write some of your thoughts here: _____

_____

_____

Behavior – How Should This Reform My Actions?

> *For this is the love of God, that we keep His commandments; and His commandments are not burdensome.*
>
> —1 John 5:3

What else but a biblical life could flow from sanctified beliefs, affections, thoughts, attitudes, priorities, and words? God has designed us such that our behaviors cannot be lastingly changed without inner change. Bible application simply *must* encompass the whole person. This wholistic approach is not always easy, but it brings the greatest glory to Christ and produces lasting change within us.

In fact, I believe that is why our Bible application typically starts well but falls off after a short time. If we attempt to change our behavior without also allowing God to transform the rest of our person through His Word, our application is doomed to be temporary at best and hypocritical at worst.

Here we see the foolishness of believing that we can rely exclusively on willpower, determination, or discipline to produce Christ-likeness in us. When did we buy into the lie that we can lead godly lives without first having a godly heart? No, my friend! God must thoroughly change us from the inside out, sanctifying us by His Spirit who indwells us (1 Thess. 5:23–24). Let us seek a lasting, significant heart change through our time in the Word, and the right behavior changes will follow naturally.

Take a few moments to consider how our passage should change your actions, and write some of your thoughts here: _____

_____

_____

Final Thoughts

I sincerely believe that it is better to live one verse than to know an entire book of the Bible. So get alone with God. Seek His face, and ask Him to show you how to apply James 1:21–25. Be specific. Be enthusiastic. Be wholistic. Let God use these truths to reshape your beliefs, affections, thoughts, attitudes, priorities, and words until you love Him above all. Surrender yourself wholly to Him, and give yourself up to the process of being made more like His Son. Take your time with our Lord, and I'll see you in the next chapter.

CHAPTER 16

MEMORIZE THE WORD

Your Word I have treasured in my heart,
That I may not sin against You.

—Ps. 119:11

AFTER ONLY 30 seconds, he can tell you the entire order of a shuffled deck of cards. Give him five minutes, and he can memorize more than 100 random dates and events, and then recite them back to you with ease. In a mere 15 minutes, he memorized and flawlessly recited 195 names and faces, a remarkable accomplishment that earned him the gold medal at the 2009 German Memory Championship.

He's a four-time Guinness World Record Holder for Memory, the world champion in numerous disciplines at the World Memory Championships, and creator of the Superbrain! memory training. He studied for and completed two Master's degrees at the same time (with top grades in both programs), and he speaks five languages. He is also the author of two books on effective memorization and a highly sought-after keynote speaker.

You might be wondering what it would be like to have a mind capable of these incredible feats of memory, but our memory expert says you already know.

Why? Because Boris Konrad wasn't born with these skills. He *learned* them.

In fact, Konrad stresses that he is simply an ordinary man, no different than you and me. Of course, his ability to set records and win memory championships required years of hard work and intentional training, but he started from the same place you and I are right now. Boris Konrad is living proof that memorizing isn't a *talent* only some of us are born with; it's a *skill* that all of us

135

can learn. And if you're willing to put in some time and effort, you can learn how to memorize anything more effectively, including Scripture.

Thankfully, the reality is that you already have a better memory than you probably realize. Consider these thoughts from Dr. Andrew M. Davis, author of *An Approach to Extended Memorization of Scripture.*

> Actually, you have a better memory than you think. Consider how many song lyrics you have memorized, many of which you don't even like! Consider how many facts of history or literature are burned in your mind. Consider how many phone numbers and addresses and significant dates are written permanently on your heart. You have a sufficiently good memory to begin memorizing Scripture. And the more you do, the better your memory will become.[17]

Be encouraged! While the thought of memorizing Scripture may seem daunting, the mind God has given you is extraordinary, just like Borio Konrad's. Your brain is sufficient for the task of Scripture memory, and that gives us hope for the next step in the Bible study process. Let's talk about memorizing the Word.

Is Scripture Memorization Really Worth It?

Before we consider some practical tips that will aid you in Scripture memorization, let's briefly consider *why* Scripture memory matters in the first place. Is memorizing Scripture a vital part of the Christian's walk with Christ, or is it just an optional add-on for overachievers? Do we really need to "hide" God's Word in our hearts if we can look up any verse on Google in less than three seconds? My prayer is that this chapter causes a deeper appreciation for Scripture memory to well up within us all. Let's examine a few reasons why this is a vital component of Bible study.

Scripture Is More Valuable Than Gold

> *I have rejoiced in the way of Your testimonies, as much as in all riches.*
>
> —Ps. 119:14

The law of Your mouth is better to me than thousands of gold and silver pieces.

—Ps. 119:72

If you were offered $5,000 for every Bible verse you memorized in the next 24 hours, how highly would you prioritize memorizing Scripture? No doubt you would drop everything to give it your full attention in order to make as much money as possible. Verses such as "Rejoice always" and "Pray without ceasing" would suddenly sound like sweet music to your ears (1 Thess. 5:16–17 for $10,000, please).

Now consider David's perspective from the above verses. I'm humbled and ashamed to think that I would make Scripture memory a greater priority to gain money when David says the Word is already more valuable than all the money in the world. Perhaps this is a heart check for us all. Do we value Scripture like David did? Do we really believe that it is better than "thousands of gold and silver pieces"? I think our answer should lead us to deep humility and repentance.

Part of the problem is that the Word seems intangible to us, which makes it difficult to recognize how much value it brings to our lives. After all, if I gave you a check for $5,000, it would make a real, tangible difference in your life. You could pay down debt, buy something you've had your eye on for a while, treat yourself to a spontaneous weekend getaway, or save it for a rainy day. No matter what you would choose to do with it, you would feel the difference of having an extra $5,000.

But Scripture memory doesn't work that way. You can spend an hour memorizing the Word and walk away without feeling differently. You can hide a verse in your heart but wonder if it will ever make an impact. If we're honest, sometimes it seems like David is exaggerating about how valuable God's Word is.

But we must change the way we value the Word. God's Word is the means by which we are saved. Even if we can't see how it's changing our lives, we can trust that God is using it to sanctify us (John 17:17). Even if it feels like it's not accomplishing anything, we know it is accomplishing God's purposes without fail because it is "living and active" (Heb. 4:12; Isa. 55:11). And we can memorize with the confidence that God's Spirit will help us remember the Word when we need it (John 14:26). God, help us value the Scriptures as highly as You do.

Scripture Is Our Sword for the Battle

Your Word have I treasured in my heart, that I may not sin against You.

—Ps. 119:11

In Ephesians 6, Paul describes the tools of spiritual warfare for the Christian. Because an unseen spiritual war rages around us every day, God has given us spiritual armor to emerge victoriously from the fight. One of the fascinating things about the armor of God is that each of the tools God has given us for spiritual warfare is *defensive* in nature—except one. You and I have only one *weapon* to fight with, and that's "the sword of the Spirit, which is the word of God" (Eph. 6:17).

Your very soul depends on how well you wield this weapon. Do not let it lay on your shelf when you need it in your heart. No soldier who wants to survive a battle enters into it unarmed or untrained, and yet a multitude of believers walk through the spiritual war of life this very way. We must learn how to wield the sword of the Spirit as Christ did (Matt. 4:1–11). Who knows what pain and anguish we may have been spared already in life if only we had made Scripture memory a greater priority.

No wonder David declares that he treasures God's Word in his heart. Your Bible translation may use the word *hid* instead of *treasured* in Psalm 119:11, but both words capture the idea well. The Hebrew word David uses here refers to hiding a priceless treasure in order to keep it safe. Since they didn't own safes in ancient times, they would hide their most valuable treasures in the ground inside their tents to keep them from being stolen (Josh. 7:21).

In other words, David is saying that because the Word is the sword that keeps him from sin, it is his most priceless and valuable treasure. As a result, he's going to hide it in the one place where it can never be stolen or taken away from him—his heart. May we also treasure the Word enough to hide it in our hearts.

Memorize Like Your Soul Depends on It

The law of his God is in his heart; his steps do not slip.

—Ps. 37:31

Have you ever paused to consider *why* we struggle so much with Scripture memory? I would humbly argue that behind our failure to memorize the Word are forces far more sinister than we typically realize.

Think of it this way. If the enemy knows that the Word is our key to standing firm against temptation, then doesn't it make sense that he would do everything possible to keep us from hiding it in our hearts? If the Word is our only sword for the battle, then doesn't it make sense that he'd try to disarm us? If the Scriptures are more valuable to our souls than the riches of this world, then wouldn't the enemy desperately resist us at this very point?

My friend, the most important thing to take away from this chapter is this: *our enemy will violently oppose us when we're about to do the very things that our souls most need.* The reason we don't like Scripture memory isn't because we're bad at memorizing; it's because we *feel* like we're bad at memorizing. The reason we don't get started isn't because Scripture memory is overwhelming; it's because it *feels* overwhelming. But let me ask you this. Are these feelings from God? Is the lethargic *feeling* we get when we're about to memorize a passage really from the Lord? No! The enemy is resisting us most where we would be helped the most.

So, memorize like your soul depends on it—because it does. Here are a few practical tips to get you started.

PRACTICAL TIPS FOR MEMORIZATION

Memorize Using a Systematic Approach

One of the biggest mistakes we make is to attempt to memorize Scripture without a system. Thankfully, there are several excellent tools and resources that can help you hide God's Word in your heart more effectively. I use the Verses app on my iPhone. It's a great tool that lets you select your Bible translation, highlight the passages you want to memorize, and memorize or review them using fun and interactive games. This and other similar apps or programs may be of great use to you.

In addition, I know several Christians who are old-school and simply run through a stack of 3x5 cards with verses written on them. Other believers memorize Scripture with their church small groups or accountability groups. The point is that there are many excellent approaches that might help you memorize Scripture. The key is to find which system works best for you and stick with it.

Memorize Passages after You've Studied Them

Another reason why we struggle to memorize Scripture is because we haven't first let it change our lives. As a general rule, "things that make sense are easier to remember than those that don't."[18] Since we find it easier to remember things *after* they have impacted us personally, it makes sense to memorize Scripture only *after* we've had a chance to study and apply it.

And because of your recent studies, James 1:21–25 is fresh in your mind. You know what each phrase or keyword means, why the passage matters, and how God has ministered to your heart through these verses. In other words, by now our passage means something to you. That will make the process of memorizing it much simpler.

As a side note, this is one of the reasons I believe we need to reexamine how we're encouraging children to memorize Bible verses. If we teach our kids to say all the words of a verse in the right order without first teaching them *why the verse is important and what it means*, I believe we're doing them a disservice. So if you have kids or work in children's Bible programs such as AWANA or Kids4Truth, let me encourage you to take time to help your kids understand the verses they're memorizing before asking them to recite them back to you. That may be a slower way for them to learn, but it will help each verse stick in their memory more effectively.

Engage the Visual Part of Your Mind

When you think about your favorite childhood memory, what is the first thing that comes to mind? Typically, the first piece of information your mind recalls is an *image* of your memory rather than *facts* about your memory. That's because our minds typically store our memories in the form of pictures, or mental images.[19]

For example, my favorite childhood memories are of playing baseball outside with my dad and siblings. But when I think back to those days, the first thoughts that come to mind aren't about the type of baseball bat we used, the color of the hat I would typically wear, or even what age I was at the time. That data simply isn't the first thing to come to mind. Rather, I *picture* myself standing in the outfield with my brother up to bat and my sister on second base. I visualize the sun setting in the background behind the big tree that we used as first base. As I'm writing these words, I can still see the cornfields all around the edge of the yard, just like in *Field of Dreams*. Mental images like these come to our minds first because our memories are primarily stored in our minds *visually*, a fact that we can use to our advantage when memorizing Scripture.

This is one additional benefit of looking up the keywords of our passage. Because we found several keywords that function as word pictures, we can visualize these concepts as we commit our verses to memory. For example, when I recite James 1:21–25, I can picture earwax clogging up the hearer's ears, the Word being implanted like a seed in soil, a forgetful man departing the mirror too soon, or the intent looking of the one who abides in the perfect law of liberty. These word pictures engage the visual part of my mind as I memorize our passage, which helps make the passage stick. The more we can visualize the concepts of our passage, the easier it will be to recall our passage when we need it.

Now It's Your Turn

God's Word is more valuable than gold. It is our sword for the battle. It helps us withstand temptation. It is the Holy Spirit's primary means of guiding us through life according to God's will. It is living, active, and powerful, and it is God's design that we treasure it enough to hide it in our hearts. Memorizing Scripture may not come naturally to you, but you are not without hope. By God's grace and with determination, you and I can learn to improve our ability to memorize Scripture. So devote yourself to memorizing our passage. Once you've hidden James 1:21–25 in your heart, I'll see you in the next chapter.

CHAPTER 17

PRAY THE WORD

But you, when you pray, go into your inner room, close your door and pray to your Father who is in secret, and your Father who sees what is done in secret will reward you.

—Matt. 6:6

IT HAS OFTEN been said that prayer is the lifeblood of the church, which means that the church will only be as vibrant, powerful, and fruitful as its praying. I also believe that our time in Bible study will only be as vibrant, powerful, and fruitful as our praying is. Thus, this particular component of Bible study demands our full attention and deserves our whole hearts.

That is another reason my Bible study was previously so powerless. For too many years I tried to study the Word apart from prayer. Now don't get me wrong. I typically started with a token prayer before cracking open the Scriptures. After all, that's what you're "supposed to do." But that was little more than a formality. In reality, I was attempting to study and obey the Word without requesting the divine grace and favor of God, and I was doomed to failure from the very beginning, as all works done in the flesh are. I lived as if prayer made no difference in my Bible study; that is, until I learned about prayer's great reward.

The Great Reward

But you, when you pray, go into your inner room, close your door and pray to your Father who is in secret, and your Father who sees what is done in secret will reward you.

—Matt. 6:6

About eight years ago, my prayer life was *really* struggling, but in God's providence I found myself studying Matthew 6. As I examined Matthew 6:6, I began to ask myself what reward God has for those who spend time in private prayer with Him. I'll be honest, I couldn't figure out what it was at first, but I knew from this verse that there was a reward for those who pray in secret. So I decided to put God's Word to the test.

I had a little storage closet in my office at work, and I decided to make that room my new prayer closet and spent a day cleaning it out. I set up a chair to sit on, started a prayer journal, and began reading books on prayer. Every day I went into my prayer closet and spent quality time in prayer with my Father, and my life hasn't been the same since. What I found was incredible. The reward Christ promises in this verse is not just simply that prayers will be answered or that needs will be met. The reward Christ promises us is intimacy with the Father Himself.

As I devoted myself to prayer, it began to feel less forced and more natural. Because no one was watching, I was free to be myself without any temptation of hypocrisy, and before I knew it, I was pouring out my heart to God as I should have been all along. I even began to look forward to my prayer time because it was becoming a delight instead of an awkward chore to check off my list. Prayer quickly became more about fellowship with God than the requests that I was bringing to Him, and I was actually experiencing the reward Christ promises us in this passage.

In time, I've seen God answer many of those prayers in amazing, even miraculous ways. As I shared earlier, I've started keeping an Answered Prayer Journal to record some of these stories because I don't want to forget the ways God has shown His power through prayer. But these answers to prayer are merely the cherry on top of the sundae. The sundae is how much more I know and love my God.

Now don't get me wrong. I have a lot to learn when it comes to prayer. But I'm so thankful for all God has taught me, and I'm in awe of His grace and majesty as He continues to open my eyes to see His glory. I pray that the next eight years brings vibrant, powerful, and fruitful times of prayer.

If your prayer life is struggling, dear friend, let me encourage you to trust Christ's words and begin cultivating the habit of spending time in private prayer. There's no greater reward than having an intimate conversation with your Creator and God, and we have that privilege through the blood of Jesus

Christ, our Great High Priest (Heb. 4:14–16). As you devote yourself to prayer, you will begin to reap its great reward—intimacy with Almighty God.

How Much Have We Forfeited?

Prayer is the lifeblood of the church, and its reward is intimacy with the Father, but I wonder how much we have forfeited by our lack of prayer? God only knows. But I believe that if God allowed us to see the blessings, mercies, graces, and gifts that we have relinquished by our lack of prayer, we would be so overwhelmed and ashamed that we would want to spend the rest of our lives on our knees.

Perhaps we must learn from the lives of those who have gone before us. The one common thread I've noticed time and again in biographies of great Christians is their love of and devotion to prayer. Brevity forbids me from telling the tales of prayer warriors such as George Muller, Hudson Taylor, Charles Spurgeon, Martin Luther, Amy Carmichael, Adoniram Judson, Elizabeth Elliot, David Brainerd, Andrew Murray, Brother Yun, and Brother Lawrence—men and women who prayed boldly and hoped greatly in their Savior. If you can find any of their biographies, I would encourage you to read of their lives and learn from their priorities. May we join them in being the prayer warriors of our day.

And if the examples of Christian history fail to persuade us, what about the example of Christ, our Great High Priest? Upon His triumphant ascension to heaven, Jesus sat down at the right hand of the Father (Heb. 1:3). But don't be mistaken. Christ did not sit down to take a rest; He sat down at the Father's right hand so He could pray for the rest of time.

> *Therefore, He is able also to save forever those who draw near to God through Him, **since He always lives to make intercession for them*** (bold emphasis added).
> —Heb. 7:25

Think of it! Of all the things Christ could devote Himself to while seated on His throne, there is one thing He has deemed most important—prayer. Let us also deem it most important.

And don't worry. God doesn't care when we stumble and fumble over our words or when we have those awkward silences where we're not quite sure what to say. He doesn't care when we forget a prayer request (He knows them all anyway) or when we sound silly. God simply isn't concerned with those things. He's concerned with our hearts. And when we do lack the words to pray, we know that the Spirit prays on our behalf with groanings that are more heartfelt than our words would have been anyway (Rom. 8:26). What a comfort this is!

With that in mind, let me encourage you to make prayer the lifeblood of your Bible study. Begin your study time with the prayer that God would open your eyes to understand His Word (Ps. 119:18). Pray that God would give you eyes to observe and interpret faithfully (2 Tim. 2:15). Pray that as you meditate, God will take His truth and make it the delight of your heart (Ps. 119:97–104). Pray for wisdom and grace as you prove yourself a doer, and pray for favor as you memorize Scripture (1 Kings 2:3; Josh. 1:8; Ps. 119:11). Finally, give thanks for all God has taught you, and pray for opportunities to pass on what you've learned to others (2 Tim. 4:1–5).

In this way, prayer isn't truly a *step* of Bible study; it is more the *spirit* in which we study. And when prayer becomes the spirit in which we *approach* the Word, it will also become the spirit in which we *do the* Word. Let's examine how this works while discussing a few ways you can pray specifically as you study the Bible.

PRACTICAL TIPS FOR PRAYER

Give Thanks for God's Word

If you woke up today with only the things you thanked God for yesterday, what would your life be like? For many of us, the reality is that our lives would be stunningly empty, a fact that reveals how stunningly ungrateful we often are. And the Bible might be what we take for granted the most, which would leave us without the Word.

Let's intentionally reverse that trend together. Now that our time of study is over, we can pause to look back on an overwhelmingly fruitful time in the Word. And what response could be more proper than to give thanks for what we've learned?

Were there any truths that particularly struck you as meaningful? Take time to thank God for them. Recently I was so struck by the overwhelming love of Christ to leave heaven to take on flesh and die in my place that I could hardly get through the passage I was studying. It humbled me, convicted me, and encouraged me. In moments like that, pause to give God thanks.

Boldly Pray for God's Grace

As we've already seen, Bible study can be a time of intense spiritual warfare. Just as God speaks to our hearts during our time in the Word, so also does the enemy whisper his lies. Understanding this is crucial to walking away from the Word with a heart set on Christ.

As you study, the enemy will bring up past sins, causing you to despair of walking in the joy of victory (Rev. 12:10). He will make the way of the cross appear too costly and the price of obedience too great (Luke 14:25–35). He will tell you that God is a liar, just as he did with Adam and Eve, and he will distort the Word either to exalt your pride or to confuse your soul (Gen. 3:4–5).

If you've studied the Bible for long, you know what this is like. All of a sudden, for reasons you can't describe, something seemingly takes the joy out of your heart and the fight out of your spirit. You're not sure why, but all of a sudden, your Bible study time has left you feeling defeated and without hope. Is that from God?

Surely not! This is our enemy at work, and his lies often cloud our judgment. Remember that God's Word is the true mirror—it will not lie to you, and it will always point you to Jesus. So when the enemy fogs the mirror with a bunch of hot air, abide in the Word until God makes His truth clear enough for you to see rightly.

It is on our knees that we must fight for our hearts, my friend. When the lies bombard your soul, take up the shield of faith, and pray for God to make the truth of the Word more real to you than the enemy's lies (Eph. 6:16). When your heart feels weak, pray for great strength (Ps. 119:28). When you don't feel like caring anymore, pray for great passion (2 Cor. 8:16). When you feel like you're invincible, pray against pride (Prov. 11:2). And when you fall on your face, pray for grace, and get back on your feet (Prov. 24:16).

Passionately Pray for God's Power

As you know by now, the life of the doer is not a life we can live in our own strength, wisdom, and power. God designed it that way. The life of the doer was always meant to be something you and I can't live on our own, which is why attempting to do the Word without praying the Word typically ends in defeat.

And yet how many of us keep spinning our wheels trying to gain spiritual traction in our own strength? How often have we tried in vain to live out the Word because we did not see that our obedience will not last long without prayer?

Just as Bible study without prayer is a hopeless endeavor, so also is obedience without prayer. After all, the prayerless Christian is a powerless Christian. Our praying—or lack of praying—has a far greater influence on our lives than we can yet understand. Only in eternity will we see what was ours by prayer and what was forfeited by our neglect.

Christ has already conquered sin, including the sin that remains within you. So why try in vain to put it to death by the flesh? Submit to Him. Pray for His power. He has already won the victory. Live in the joyful freedom that His obedience has obtained for you and embrace the life of the doer. After all, it is the life God created you for.

Now It's Your Turn

Before we move on to our final step of the Bible study process, let me encourage you to take some time to be alone with the Father. Bow yourself in humility before Him. Settle in your heart that He alone is Lord and King. Surrender yourself to Him without holding back. Confess your sins to Him in full. He is gracious and kind, not vengeful and mean. Ask boldly for the grace and strength you need for today. Let tomorrow worry about itself. Pray in faith that He hears you and has your best interest at heart. The Father is your Good Shepherd. His care for You is perfect, and His plans for You are good (Ps. 23).

Pray through our passage for yourself and those you love. Consider all that God has taught you and ask Him to make these truths a living reality in your life. Commit yourself to be an effectual doer rather than a forgetful hearer. Pray in faith that God will bless those who prove themselves doers of His Word. Take your time praying through our passage, and when you're ready, I'll see you in the next chapter.

CHAPTER 18

TEACH THE WORD

Preach the Word; be ready in season and *out of season; reprove, rebuke, exhort, with great patience and instruction.*

—2 Tim. 4:2

WE'VE COME A long way together, my friend. We've analyzed the context of James 1:21–25, looked up the keywords, interpreted our passage, meditated on why it matters, applied it wholistically to our lives, memorized it, and prayed it over ourselves and others. But there's one thing left for us to do—teach it to others.

You see, the things we've learned together were not meant to be *hoarded*; they were meant to be *shared*. For thousands of years, God's Word has been chugging along the railroad of history, changing lives and redeeming souls, and we were never meant to be the final stop on its journey.

Who knows where God intends for His Word to go next through you? Who knows how many souls might be saved by your willingness to share what you've learned, and who can fathom how much the Spirit can do with one person who shares without fail what they've seen in the Scriptures? And yet few of us are willing to be so intentional. Oh, God, forgive us! Lord, stir us up to be men and women who delight to teach Your Word to others. Let's begin by examining a few reasons to be encouraged that you can do this, even if public speaking isn't your thing.

Most Bible Teaching Is Informal

Many Christians who love Jesus tremble at the idea of sharing Scripture with others because they assume it requires public speaking. As a result, for most of us, the thought of teaching the Word seems intimidating and overwhelming. But be encouraged! Most Bible teaching happens in normal, everyday conversations like the ones you and I have every day.

You don't need to preach a Sunday sermon or lead a small group to teach the Word. You can talk about the Bible around your dinner table, at your kids' soccer game, or even when you bump into a friend at the grocery store. You can teach the Word "when you sit in your house and when you walk by the way and when you lie down and when you rise up" (Deut. 6:7). All you need is a passion for the Word and someone who is willing to listen.

We Naturally Talk about the Things We Love

Generally speaking, we talk about the things we love most. The fiancé shares about their lover, the grandparents gladly go on about their grandchildren, and the artist expresses their enjoyment of their craft. But if this premise is true, shouldn't it alarm us that we talk so little about God's Word?

Even in our conversations with fellow believers, doesn't the majority of our talking center on trivial matters such as sporting events, politics, and TV shows? As soon as a worship service or small group Bible study ends, why do we revert so quickly to talking about the news or swapping jokes when the living and active Word has just been explained to us (Heb. 4:12)? I fear that perhaps we even spend more time gossiping behind one another's backs than we do sharing the Word to one another's faces. My friend, we must ask God to search our hearts here. If our conversations reveal what we love most, then what do your words say about you?

If we talk about the things we love, then the Word will spread through our homes, our communities, and our churches when we fall in love with it again. I pray that already a deeper love for the truth has been kindled in your heart and that its flame only grows stronger as you continue to study the Word for yourself.

We Confidently Talk about the Things We Know

Have you ever been in a conversation where you had no idea what everyone else was talking about? Perhaps everyone was laughing at an inside joke you weren't aware of. Or maybe a group of coworkers were talking about their jobs in a way you couldn't quite follow. Whatever the case, most of us find these situations awkward because we don't know enough about the subject to contribute to the conversation.

The reality is that we typically remain silent when we don't know what we're talking about, and our lack of understanding has also kept us silent with the Word. But this no longer has to be the case. You and I now understand how to study the Word for ourselves, which means we're already 95 percent equipped to teach it well. The only thing left for us to consider is how to explain what we've learned in a way that's engaging. Here are a few questions that might help you as you consider how to share what you've learned from James 1:21–25.

QUESTIONS TO CONSIDER

Which Word Pictures Struck Me Most Powerfully?

Because the word pictures of a passage often stick in our minds best, it is helpful to consider how we might incorporate them as we explain our passage. So feel free to look back through your notes on the keywords in Chapters 10–11, and consider which word pictures most helped you understand what James is saying. The word pictures that resonate with you most powerfully will be the ones you talk about most passionately.

When I'm talking with others about James 1:21–25, I often use word pictures like the earwax, the forgetful man in the mirror, the two types of looking, and the idea of the Word being implanted. These word pictures have impacted my life personally, so I find it quite natural to share about them as I teach.

Did Any Analogies or Stories Come to Mind?

In addition to word pictures, you might want to incorporate analogies or stories that you thought of as you studied our passage. Perhaps you thought of a time you left the mirror too quickly and were embarrassed by your appearance later that day. Maybe you thought of a gardening analogy that illustrates how important it is for the implanted word to be placed in good soil. Or perhaps you have a creative way to illustrate the two types of looking in our passage and why they matter.

Every time I study a passage, I try to think of at least one analogy or story that can help me creatively illustrate the truths I've just learned. Try to think of your own analogy for our passage and how you might incorporate it as you tell someone else about what you've learned.

Did This Passage Remind Me of Another Passage?

One passage of Scripture will often point us to another passage. Sometimes that happens because your passage is quoting another passage word for word, and at other times a word or phrase simply jogs your memory of another verse. Either way, if these connections have been helpful for you as you studied, then they'll be helpful for you as you teach.

Our passage reminds me of two other parts of the Bible. First, every time I think of "the implanted word," Christ's parable of the Sower and the seed comes to mind (Mark 4:1–20). And second, the emphasis on hearing and doing the Word reminds me of Christ's ending to the Sermon on the Mount.

> Therefore **everyone who hears these words of Mine and acts on them,** may be compared to a **wise man** who built his house on the rock. And the rain fell, and the floods came, and the winds blew and slammed against that house; and yet it did not fall, for it had been founded on the rock. **Everyone who hears these words of Mine and does not act on them,** will be like a **foolish man** who built his house on the sand. The rain fell, and the floods came, and the winds blew and slammed against that house; and it fell—and great was its fall (bold emphasis added).
>
> —Matt. 7:24–27

Perhaps different passages came to mind for you as you studied James 1:21–25. Whatever they were, it is helpful to consider how you might incorporate them as you talk with someone about what you've learned.

What Wasn't Clear to Me at First?

As I study a passage, I take mental notes about the things that aren't immediately clear to me so I can make sure to explain them to others. After all, if something wasn't clear to me at first, it's likely that someone else might be confused on that same point as well.

There were two parts of our passage, that at first, I couldn't understand. First, I couldn't grasp why James used the analogy of a male looking in the mirror as opposed to a female. Second, it took me a while to understand why James used two different words for *looking* in our passage. As result, I try to explain these parts clearly and intentionally every time I share about James 1:21–25.

What Was I Convicted of as I Studied?

When I'm preparing to teach the Word, I always pause to consider where the passage convicted me most. James 1:21–25 deeply convicted me of all the times I've heard the Word clearly, seen something I've needed to change, and then walked away like the forgetful man who was looking in the mirror. I have been a hearer of the Word far more often than I'd like to admit, and that means that others probably have too. With that in mind, I want to teach the Word in such a way that I'm humbly and authentically sharing where I tend to fall short and how I've found hope and solutions in this passage.

What Does This Passage Tell Us about Jesus?

Some Bible passages speak of Christ overtly, and others seem to require more work on our part. But every passage in the Bible points us to Christ as the object of our hope, comfort, and faith. It is often helpful to consider what we can learn about Him as we think of how to share the Word with others.

In our passage, we see the ongoing internal struggle we have between hearing and doing the Word. Every true Christian wants to live in obedience to the Word, but for some reason we all have this dangerous tendency to walk away from the mirror without changing. We've all failed to play the role of the doer at times and settled for hearing only. We've all known ways we should live differently in light of the Bible but neglected to do so. Every one of us has fallen repeatedly in this area, but this is where Jesus comes in. Jesus is the perfect Doer of the Word.

Think of it! Jesus is the only One who *never* failed to do the Word. He was tempted, yes, but He never sinned (Heb. 4:15). He never read a passage of Scripture and felt conviction like we do. Every time He looked in the mirror of the Word, He saw only perfection—the kind of perfection you and I could only dream of. He lived His whole life abiding in the perfect law of liberty, and then He fulfilled it in our place (Matt. 5:17).

Then on the cross, Jesus willingly took on our plight and exchanged places with us. He took our sin upon Himself and freely offered us His righteousness. He took our guilt upon His shoulders so we could be declared innocent. He took the wrath of God in our place, and now He offers us mercy. He became separated from God so that through Him we might be united with God. He died in our place so He could offer us eternal life.

This is the gospel, my friend. Christ has come to be the Doer of the Word that you and I have so often failed to be. And now He freely offers Himself as the Savior, Redeemer, Lord, Deliverer, and Friend of all who will trust in Him. If you have never placed your faith and hope in Jesus Christ, then fall on your face and cry to Him for salvation today. His love is infinite, His grace is sufficient, and His power is mighty to save you at this very moment.

Your Turn

Here is your final homework assignment. If I were to ask you what God has been teaching you lately through the Word, how would you explain James 1:21–25 to me? What convicted you as you studied? Which word pictures, analogies, and other passages might help you explain it well? What was most confusing to you at first? And how could you use our passage to point me to Jesus?

Take your time on this part. The beautiful thing about teaching the Word is that the harder you work to explain the passage well, the more God continues to teach *you* during the process. Feel free to make notes or write thoughts in the space provided until you have a good idea of how you would explain James 1:21–25. Once you're finished, pray for God to give you at least one opportunity to share what you've learned with someone else this week, and be on the lookout for how He plans to use you to spread His Word to others.

May God bless you as you prepare to share what you've learned!

Your Explanation of James 1:21–25

_____

_____

_____

_____

_____

_____

_____

_____

_____

_____

_____

_____

_____

_____

_____

_____

_____

_____

_____

_____

_____

_____

_____

_____

_____

_____

_____

_____

CHAPTER 19

CLOSING THOUGHTS

I thank my God in all my remembrance of you.
—Phil. 1:3

THIS BOOK WASN'T meant for the mildly interested or half-hearted Christian, so if you've made it this far, *thank you*. Thank you for being willing to persevere. But you and I both know that our journey has only just begun. I pray that as we seek God through His Word, we will all become Christ-like spouses, parents, coworkers, church leaders, and community influencers who know, live, and share God's truth.

My only request of you is that you pass along these truths to someone else who needs to hear them. The truth was never meant to stop with you and me, so together let's make our lives about equipping those around us to study, practice, and teach the Word.

Study. Practice. Teach.

These three words are more than a just catchphrase or slogan; they're a way of life. They represent the life I want to lead, the man I'm striving to be, and the legacy I want to leave behind. I hope you'll join me.

Ben Williams
Macon, North Carolina

ACKNOWLEDGMENTS

WRITING A BOOK is a team sport, and I was blessed beyond measure by the team God surrounded me with. I couldn't have made this journey without them. First, I want to thank my beautiful wife, Cara, for her consistent encouragement and unwavering support. Cara served as my primary proofreader, and without her encouragement, critiques, and input, this book would simply not be what it is. Honey, I'm humbled to think of how many times you served me during the writing process. You are more than I deserve. I'm thankful for you, and I'm proud to be your husband.

In addition, I want to thank my daughter, Aletheia. I had toyed with this manuscript for two years before she was born, but when she arrived, I knew this was a project I had to finish. I long for my daughter to know God deeply through His Word, and I pray that these words equip her to fall more in love with God than I have and to do more for the cause of Christ than I ever will.

In addition, I'm humbled when I think of how thankful I am for the feedback I got from various proofreaders along the way. Mom, thanks for paving the way for me through your own writing and sharing what you've learned along the way. My proofreaders—Matt and Sarie Glick, Terry and Lynn Breen, Morgan Robinette, Brandon Shaffer, and Shirey Little—I appreciate each of you deeply for taking the time to read this book and help me sharpen my thoughts. Many of your suggestions were incorporated into the final draft, and I'm profoundly thankful for your wisdom and direction. In addition, I'm deeply indebted to my mentor, Dr. Jim Shaddix, for urging me to "go for it" once the manuscript was finished.

Finally, from the very beginning, I knew I wanted to work with a publishing company that is unashamedly Christian and upholds honest business practices. I couldn't have found a better publisher to work with than the team at Lucid Books. They have been a joy to work with, and their professionalism, expertise, and communication have made this book far better than it was in its original form. I would recommend them without reservation to any aspiring Christian author. To the team at Lucid Books, thank you for your dedication to this project, and congratulations on a job well done!

APPENDIX A

ANSWERS TO EXERCISES IN CHAPTER 5

There are five differences between the two pictures.

 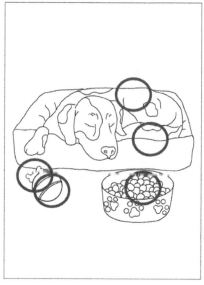

How Many Squares Do You See?

Answer: 30

16 squares are 1x1

9 squares are 2x2

4 squares are 3x3

1 square is 4x4

Can You Find Both of the Women in This Picture?

Answer: The young woman is looking over her right shoulder (to the upper left of the image) and the old woman is looking down to the left.

Spot the Differences

Let's make it a bit harder this time.
Can you find 8 differences between these two pictures?

Spot Eight Differences

One final test. Can you find 8 differences below?

APPENDIX B

BIBLE STUDY RESOURCES

I've intentionally saved this part for last because it's the least necessary. As long as you have your Bible, the Holy Spirit, and a willing heart, you can study and obey the Bible. However, there are some excellent tools and resources that can aid us as we seek to understand the Word. Listed below are several categories of resources, many of which were used in the process of writing this book.

Concordances and Lexicons

The New Strong's Expanded Exhaustive Concordance of the Bible – James Strong
Young's Analytical Concordance of the Bible – Robert Young
The Brown-Driver-Briggs Hebrew and English Lexicon – Francis Brown, S. R. Driver, and Charles A. Briggs
Theological Dictionary of the New Testament – Gerhard Kittel and Gerhard Friedrich
Theological Dictionary of the Old Testament – G. Johannes Botterweck, Helmer Ringgren, et al.

Additional Books about How to Study the Bible

Grasping God's Word – J. Scott Duvall and J. Daniel Hays
How to Read the Bible Book by Book – Gordon D. Fee and Douglas Stuart
How to Read the Bible for All It's Worth – Gordon D. Fee and Douglas Stuart
Living by the Book – Howard G. Hendricks, William D. Hendricks, et al.

Surveys of the Bible (Great for an Overview)

An Introduction to the Old Testament – Tremper Longman III and Raymond B. Dillard
The Promise and the Blessing – Michael A. Harbin
A Survey of the Old Testament – Andrew E. Hill and John H. Walton
New Testament Survey – Merrill C. Tenney
An Introduction to the New Testament – D. A. Carson and Douglas J. Moo

Commentary on the New Testament Use of the Old Testament – D. A. Carson and G. K. Beale

Archaeological Commentary on the Bible – Gonzalo Báez-Camargo

Atlases

The New Moody Atlas of the Bible – Barry J. Beitzel

Holman Bible Atlas – Thomas V. Brisco

Zondervan Atlas of the Bible – Carl G. Rasmussen

Bible Dictionaries

Zondervan's Pictorial Bible Dictionary – J. D. Douglas and Merrill C. Tenney

The Baker Illustrated Bible Background Commentary – J. Scott Duvall and J. Daniel Hays

The New Unger's Bible Dictionary – Merrill F. Unger

Commentary Sets

Christ-Centered Exposition Commentary Series

Expositor's Bible Commentary

Holman Old Testament Commentary

Holman New Testament Commentary

New American Commentary

New International Commentary on the New Testament

New International Commentary on the Old Testament

NIV Application Commentary

Pillar New Testament Commentary

Preaching the Word Commentary

Bible Study Software Programs

Blue Letter Bible – www.blueletterbible.org

E-Sword – www.e-sword.net

Logos – By far the best, but it can be very expensive (visit www.logos.com for details on pricing)

The Word – www.theword.net

Other Internet Helps

Bible Hub – www.biblehub.com

BiblicalTraining – www.biblicaltraining.org

Desiring God – www.desiringgod.org

Grace to You – www.gty.org

Look at the Book – www.desiringgod.org/labs

Precept Austin – www.preceptaustin.org

Radical – www.radical.net

RightNow Media – www.rightnowmedia.org

BibleProject – www.thebibleproject.com

APPENDIX C

KEYWORD RESOURCES

Below is a list of resources used to determine the meaning of each keyword listed in Chapter 11: Looking Up Keywords – Part 2. You'll notice that I never take only one dictionary or website at its word. I always try to find a minimum of three credible sources to confirm the meaning of a keyword.

For the sake of our study, I've limited my research to only free online resources so you can follow along with these keyword studies without spending any money. However, if you're interested in purchasing your own keyword resources (which often provide more in-depth analysis), Appendix B: Bible Study Resources provide you a list of concordances and lexicons that I recommend.

Verse 21

"Putting Aside"
1. Precept Austin's commentary on James 1:21, https://www.preceptaustin.org/james_121
2. Bible Hub's Greek Lexicon, https://biblehub.com/greek/659.htm
3. StudyLight.org Greek Lexicon, https://www.studylight.org/lexicons/eng/greek/659.html

"Filthiness"
1. Precept Austin's commentary on James 1:21, https://www.preceptaustin.org/james_121
2. William Barclay's Daily Bible Study on James, https://www.studylight.org/commentaries/eng/dsb/james-1.html
3. Bible Hub's Greek Lexicon, https://biblehub.com/greek/4507b.htm

"Remains"
1. Precept Austin's commentary on James 1:21, https://www.preceptaustin.org/james_121
2. Bible Hub's Greek Lexicon, https://biblehub.com/greek/4050.htm

3. StudyLight.org Greek Lexicon, https://www.studylight.org/lexicons/eng/greek/4050.html

"Wickedness"

1. Precept Austin's commentary on James 1:21, https://www.preceptaustin.org/james_121
2. Bible Hub's Greek Lexicon, https://biblehub.com/greek/2549.htm
3. StudyLight.org Greek Lexicon, https://www.studylight.org/lexicons/eng/greek/2549.html

"Humility"

1. Precept Austin's commentary on James 1:21, https://www.preceptaustin.org/james_121
2. Bible Hub's Greek Lexicon, https://biblehub.com/greek/4240.htm
3. William Barclay's Daily Bible Study on James, https://www.studylight.org/commentaries/eng/dsb/james-1.html
4. StudyLight.org Greek Lexicon, https://www.studylight.org/lexicons/eng/greek/4240.html

"Receive"

1. Precept Austin's commentary on James 1:21, https://www.preceptaustin.org/james_121
2. Bible Hub's Greek Lexicon, https://biblehub.com/greek/1209.htm
3. StudyLight.org Greek Lexicon, https://www.studylight.org/lexicons/eng/greek/1209.html

"Word"

1. Precept Austin's commentary on James 1:21, https://www.preceptaustin.org/james_121
2. William Barclay's Daily Bible Study on James, https://www.studylight.org/commentaries/eng/dsb/james-1.html
3. Bible Hub's Greek Lexicon, https://biblehub.com/greek/3056.htm

"Able"

1. Precept Austin's commentary on James 1:21, https://www.preceptaustin.org/james_121

2. Studylight.org Commentaries on the Epistle of James, https://www.study-light.org/commentary/james/1-21.html

3. Bible Hub's Greek Lexicon, https://biblehub.com/greek/1410.htm

4. StudyLight.org Greek Lexicon, https://www.studylight.org/lexicons/eng/greek/1410.html

"Save"

1. Precept Austin's commentary on James 1:21, https://www.preceptaustin.org/james_121

2. Studylight.org Commentaries on the Epistle of James, https://www.study-light.org/commentary/james/1-21.html

3. Bible Hub's Greek Lexicon, https://biblehub.com/greek/4982.htm

4. StudyLight.org Greek Lexicon, https://www.studylight.org/lexicons/eng/greek/4982.html

"Souls"

1. Precept Austin's commentary on James 1:21, https://www.preceptaustin.org/james_121

2. Studylight.org Commentaries on the Epistle of James, https://www.study-light.org/commentary/james/1-21.html

3. Bible Hub's Greek Lexicon, https://biblehub.com/greek/5590.htm

4. StudyLight.org Greek Lexicon, https://www.studylight.org/lexicons/eng/greek/5590.html

Verse 22

"Prove"

1. Precept Austin's commentary on James 1:22–24, https://www.preceptaustin.org/james_122-24

2. Studylight.org Commentaries on the Epistle of James, https://www.study-light.org/commentary/james/1-22.html

3. Bible Hub's Greek Lexicon, https://biblehub.com/greek/1096.htm

"Doers"

1. Precept Austin's commentary on James 1:22–24, https://www.preceptaustin.org/james_122-24

2. Studylight.org Commentaries on the Epistle of James, https://www.study-light.org/commentary/james/1-22.html

3. Bible Hub's Greek Lexicon, https://biblehub.com/greek/4163.htm

"Hearers"

1. Precept Austin's commentary on James 1:22–24, https://www.preceptaus-tin.org/james_122-24

2. Studylight.org Commentaries on the Epistle of James, https://www.study-light.org/commentary/james/1-22.html

3. Bible Hub's Greek Lexicon, https://biblehub.com/greek/202.htm

4. StudyLight.org Greek Lexicon, https://www.studylight.org/lexicons/eng/greek/202.html

"Delude"

1. Precept Austin's commentary on James 1:22–24, https://www.preceptaus-tin.org/james_122-24

2. Studylight.org Commentaries on the Epistle of James, https://www.study-light.org/commentary/james/1-22.html

3. Bible Hub's Greek Lexicon, https://biblehub.com/greek/3884.htm

Verse 23

"Man"

1. Precept Austin's commentary on James 1:22–24, https://www.preceptaus-tin.org/james_122-24

2. Studylight.org Commentaries on the Epistle of James, https://www.study-light.org/commentary/james/1-23.html

3. Bible Hub's Greek Lexicon, https://biblehub.com/greek/435.htm

"Looks"

1. Precept Austin's commentary on James 1:22–24, https://www.preceptaus-tin.org/james_122-24

2. Studylight.org Commentaries on the Epistle of James, https://www.study-light.org/commentary/james/1-23.html

3. Bible Hub's Greek Lexicon, https://biblehub.com/greek/2657.htm

4. StudyLight.org Greek Lexicon, https://www.studylight.org/lexicons/eng/greek/2657.html

"Natural Face"

1. Precept Austin's commentary on James 1:22–24, https://www.preceptaustin.org/james_122-24
2. Studylight.org Commentaries on the Epistle of James, https://www.studylight.org/commentary/james/1-23.html
3. Bible Hub's Greek Lexicon – "natural," https://biblehub.com/greek/1078.htm
4. Bible Hub's Greek Lexicon – "face," https://biblehub.com/greek/4383.htm

"Mirror"

1. Precept Austin's commentary on James 1:22–24, https://www.preceptaustin.org/james_122-24
2. Studylight.org Commentaries on the Epistle of James, https://www.studylight.org/commentary/james/1-23.html
3. Bible Hub's Greek Lexicon, https://biblehub.com/greek/2072.htm

Verse 24

"Has Looked"

1. Precept Austin's commentary on James 1:22–24, https://www.preceptaustin.org/james_122-24
2. Studylight.org Commentaries on the Epistle of James, https://www.studylight.org/commentary/james/1-24.html
3. Bible Hub's Greek Lexicon, https://biblehub.com/greek/2657.htm
4. StudyLight.org Greek Lexicon, https://www.studylight.org/lexicons/eng/greek/2657.html

"Gone Away"

1. Precept Austin's commentary on James 1:22–24, https://www.preceptaustin.org/james_122-24
2. Studylight.org Commentaries on the Epistle of James, https://www.studylight.org/commentary/james/1-24.html

3. Bible Hub's Greek Lexicon, https://biblehub.com/greek/565.htm

"Immediately"

1. Precept Austin's commentary on James 1:22–24, https://www.preceptaustin.org/james_122-24
2. Studylight.org Commentaries on the Epistle of James, https://www.studylight.org/commentary/james/1-24.html
3. Bible Hub's Greek Lexicon, https://biblehub.com/greek/2112.htm
4. StudyLight.org Greek Lexicon, https://www.studylight.org/lexicons/eng/greek/2112.html

"Forgotten"

1. Precept Austin's commentary on James 1:22–24, https://www.preceptaustin.org/james_122-24
2. Studylight.org Commentaries on the Epistle of James, https://www.studylight.org/commentary/james/1-24.html
3. Bible Hub's Greek Lexicon, https://biblehub.com/greek/1950.htm

Verse 25

"Looks Intently"

1. Precept Austin's commentary on James 1:25, https://www.preceptaustin.org/james_125
2. Studylight.org Commentaries on the Epistle of James, https://www.studylight.org/commentary/james/1-25.html
3. Bible Hub's Greek Lexicon, https://biblehub.com/greek/3879.htm
4. StudyLight.org Greek Lexicon, https://www.studylight.org/lexicons/eng/greek/3879.html

"Perfect"

1. Precept Austin's commentary on James 1:25, https://www.preceptaustin.org/james_125
2. Studylight.org Commentaries on the Epistle of James, https://www.studylight.org/commentary/james/1-25.html
3. Bible Hub's Greek Lexicon, https://biblehub.com/greek/5046.htm

"Law"

1. Precept Austin's commentary on James 1:25, https://www.preceptaustin.org/james_125
2. Studylight.org Commentaries on the Epistle of James, https://www.studylight.org/commentary/james/1-25.html
3. Bible Hub's Greek Lexicon, https://biblehub.com/greek/3551.htm

"Liberty"

1. Precept Austin's commentary on James 1:25, https://www.preceptaustin.org/james_125
2. Studylight.org Commentaries on the Epistle of James, https://www.studylight.org/commentary/james/1-25.html
3. Bible Hub's Greek Lexicon, https://biblehub.com/greek/1657.htm
4. StudyLight.org Greek Lexicon, https://www.studylight.org/lexicons/eng/greek/1657.html

"Abides"

1. Precept Austin's commentary on James 1:25, https://www.preceptaustin.org/james_125
2. Studylight.org Commentaries on the Epistle of James, https://www.studylight.org/commentary/james/1-25.html
3. Bible Hub's Greek Lexicon, https://biblehub.com/greek/3887.htm

"Forgetful"

1. Precept Austin's commentary on James 1:25, https://www.preceptaustin.org/james_125
2. Studylight.org Commentaries on the Epistle of James, https://www.studylight.org/commentary/james/1-25.html
3. Bible Hub's Greek Lexicon, https://biblehub.com/greek/1953.htm
4. StudyLight.org Greek Lexicon, https://www.studylight.org/lexicons/eng/greek/1953.html

"Effectual Doer"

1. Precept Austin's commentary on James 1:25, https://www.preceptaustin.org/james_125

2. Studylight.org Commentaries on the Epistle of James, https://www.study-light.org/commentary/james/1-25.html

3. Bible Hub's Greek Lexicon – "effectual," https://biblehub.com/greek/2041.htm

4. Bible Hub's Greek Lexicon – "doer," https://biblehub.com/greek/4163.htm

5. StudyLight.org Greek Lexicon, https://www.studylight.org/lexicons/eng/greek/2041.html

6. StudyLight.org Greek Lexicon, https://www.studylight.org/lexicons/eng/greek/4163.html

"Blessed"

1. Precept Austin's commentary on James 1:25, https://www.preceptaustin.org/james_125

2. Studylight.org Commentaries on the Epistle of James, https://www.study-light.org/commentary/james/1-25.html

3. Bible Hub's Greek Lexicon, https://biblehub.com/greek/3107.htm

ENDNOTES

1. Andrew Murray, *Absolute Surrender and Other Addresses* (CreateSpace Independent Publishing Platform, 2017), 63.

2. A. W. Tozer, *That Incredible Christian* (Chicago: Moody Publishers, 2018), 96.

3. Pete Briscoe, "The Key to Living the Christian Life," November 22, 2016, https://benttree.org/editorial/the-key-to-living-the-christian-life/.

4. For an excellent treatment of Christ's letter to the church at Laodicea, see John MacArthur, *Because the Time Is Near: John MacArthur Explains the Book of Revelation* (Chicago: Moody Publishers, 2007), 96–103.

5. For further discussion of the authorship of James, see Douglas J. Moo, *The Letter of James (The Pillar New Testament Commentary)*, (Grand Rapids, MI: Eerdmans, 2000), 9–11.

6. Cited in George Barlow and Robert Tuck, *I & II Timothy, Titus, Philemon, Hebrews, James (The Preacher's Complete Homiletic Commentary)*, (New York: Funk & Wagnalls Company, 1892), 484–485.

7. Ibid., 485.

8. My guess is that James wrote his letter in the early 40s AD.

9. Taken from a transcript of David Platt's sermon, "The Cross and Christian Discipline – Part 2," delivered June 9, 2013, https://radical.net/message/the-cross-and-christian-discipline-part-2/.

10. Dr. Thomas L. Constable, "Notes on James," 2023 Edition, SonicLight.com, https://www.planobiblechapel.org/tcon/notes/html/nt/james/james.htm.

11. "Meditate," Online Etymology Dictionary, accessed May 10, 2023, https://www.etymonline.com/word/meditate.

12. For a thorough and encouraging treatment of biblical meditation, see Thomas Watson, *Meditation: A Christian on the Mount* (Peterbourough, Ontario: H&E Publishing, 2021).

13. Results based on a search of the word *meditate* in Logos Bible Software using the NASB 1995 translation. Interestingly, the word *meditate* does not occur in the New Testament.

14. John C. Maxwell, *Attitude 101: What Every Leader Needs to Know* (Nashville: TN, Thomas Nelson, 2015), 36.

15. As told by John C. Maxwell in *Developing the Leader within You* (Nashville: TN, Thomas Nelson, 1993), 31.

16. Paul Petrone, "You Speak (at Least) 7,000 Words a Day. Here's How to Make Them Count," LinkedIn Learning Blog, August 17, 2017, https://www.linkedin.com/business/learning/blog/career-success-tips/you-speak-at-least-7-000-words-a-day-here-s-how-to-make-them.

17. Dr. Andrew Davis, *An Approach to Extended Memorization of Scripture*, accessed May 10, 2023, https://scripturememory.com/downloadables/andrewdavis.pdf.

18. Kyle Buchanan, "How to Memorize 10x Faster," Memorize Academy, accessed April 4, 2023, https://www.memorize.academy/blog/how-to-memorize-10x-faster. For additional training in memorization, I encourage you to consider taking Buchanan's online course, "The 3 Essential Techniques," which can be found on his website at https://www.memorize.academy/memory-training-courses.

19. According to the BetterHelp Editorial Team, as much as 80 percent of our learning is visual in nature. See "Visual Memory and How It May Be Improved," BetterHelp, December 7, 2022, https://www.betterhelp.com/advice/memory/what-is-a-visual-memory-and-how-does-it-affect-us/

Printed in the USA
CPSIA information can be obtained
at www.ICGtesting.com
LVHW022020290923
759527LV00007B/668